CREATIVE
FAMILY FAVOURITES

CREATIVE
FAMILY FAVOURITES

FRANCES CLEARY

Dolphin Publications

This edition specially produced for
Dolphin Publications,
Bridge Mills Business Park,
Langley Road South
Pendleton
Salford, M6 6EL

First published by Dolphin Publications in 1993
and exclusive to them in the UK.

© 1993 Anness Publishing Limited
Boundary Row Studios
1 Boundary Row
London SE1 8HP

ISBN 1-873762-66-6

Editorial Director: Joanna Lorenz
Project Editor: Carole Clements
Copy Editors: Norma MacMillan and Penny David
Designer: Sheila Volpe
Photographer: Amanda Heywood
Food Styling: Frances Cleary, Carole Handslip,
steps by Nicola Fowler

Printed and bound in Hong Kong

ACKNOWLEDGEMENTS

For their assistance in the production of this book the publishers wish to thank:

American Country Collections Limited
28 Baker Street
Weybridge, Surrey KT13 8AU

British Gas North Thames
North Thames House
London Road
Staines, Middlesex TW18 4AE

M.C. Typeset Limited
The Barn, Woodbank House
Rochester Road
Wouldham, Kent ME1 3RB

Magimix
115A High Street
Godalming, Surrey GU7 1AQ

Prestige
Prestige House
22–26 High Street
Egham, Surrey TW20 9DU

Staks
24 The Waterglade Centre
The Broadway, Ealing
London W5 2ND

CONTENTS

~

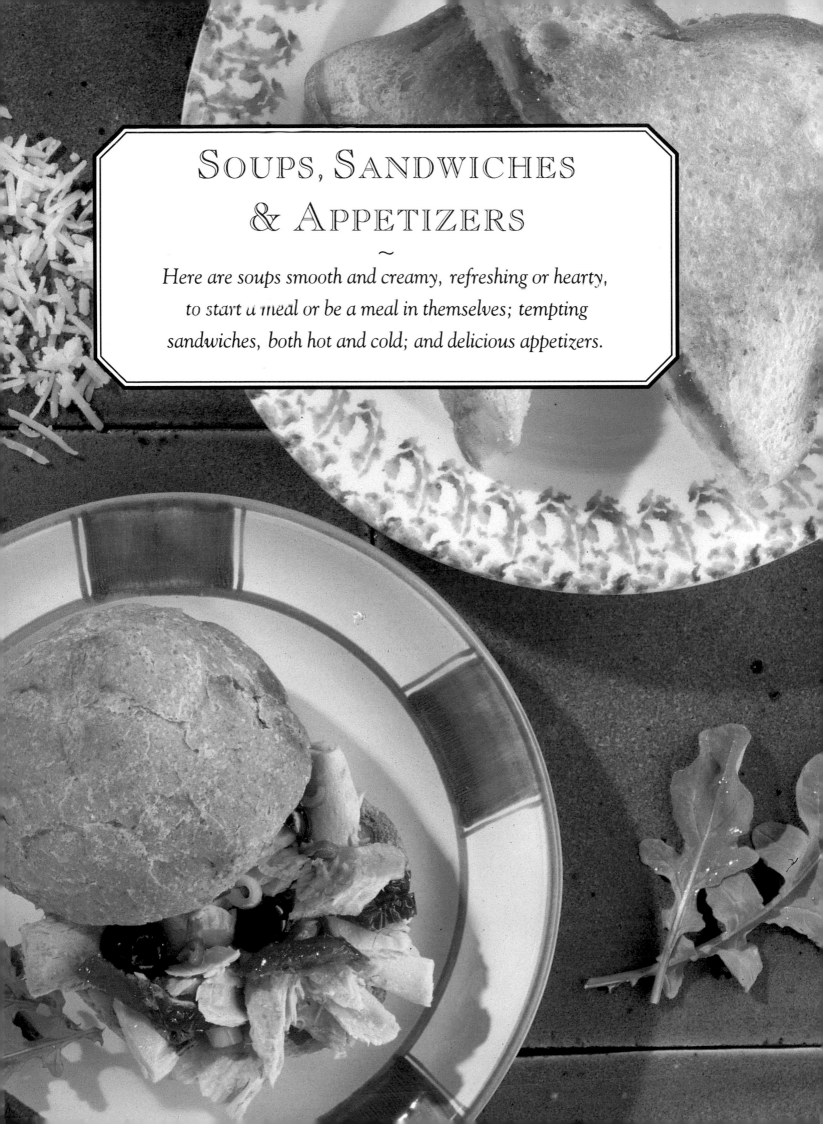

SOUPS, SANDWICHES & APPETIZERS

~

*Here are soups smooth and creamy, refreshing or hearty,
to start a meal or be a meal in themselves; tempting
sandwiches, both hot and cold; and delicious appetizers.*

Carrot Soup

Serves 6

1 oz (30 g) butter or margarine

1 onion, chopped

1 celery stick, chopped

1 medium-sized potato, chopped

1½ lb (700 g) carrots, chopped

2 tsp grated fresh root ginger

2 pt (1.25 litres) chicken stock

3 fl oz (85 ml) whipping cream

¼ teaspoon grated nutmeg

salt and pepper

1 ▼ Combine the butter or margarine, onion and celery and cook until softened, about 5 minutes.

2 Stir in the potato, carrots, ginger and stock. Bring to the boil. Reduce the heat to low, cover the pan and simmer 20 minutes.

3 ▲ Pour the soup into a food processor or blender and process until smooth. Alternatively, use a vegetable mill to purée the soup. Return the soup to the pan. Stir in the cream and nutmeg and add salt and pepper to taste. Reheat gently for serving.

Minty Pea Soup

Serves 6

1 oz (30 g) butter or margarine

1 onion, chopped

1 small head of lettuce, shredded

2 lb (900 g) shelled fresh green peas or frozen peas, thawed

2½ pt (1.5 litres) chicken stock

3 tbsp chopped fresh mint

salt and pepper

6 fl oz (175 ml) whipping cream

fresh mint sprigs, for garnishing

~ VARIATION ~

To serve cold, refrigerate the puréed soup until thoroughly chilled, 3–4 hours. Stir all the cream into the soup just before serving, or keep some to swirl over each serving.

1 ▲ Melt the butter or margarine in a large saucepan. Add the onion and cook until softened, about 5 minutes.

2 ▲ Stir in the lettuce, peas, stock and mint. Bring to the boil. Reduce the heat to low, cover the pan and simmer 15 minutes.

3 Pour the soup into a blender or food processor and process until smooth. Alternatively, purée the soup in a vegetable mill. Return the puréed soup to the pan. Season to taste.

4 ▲ Stir in two-thirds of the cream and reheat gently. Ladle into bowls and serve with the remaining cream. For a decorative effect, pour a scant tablespoon of cream in a spiral design into the centre of each serving, or stir it in and garnish with sprigs of mint.

Carrot Soup (top), Minty Pea Soup

Spicy Mixed Bean Soup

SERVES 8

12 oz (350 g) dried black or red kidney beans, soaked overnight

3½ pt (2 litres) water

6 garlic cloves, crushed

12 oz (350 g) dried haricot or white beans, soaked overnight

6 tbsp balsamic or white wine vinegar

4 chilli peppers, seeded and chopped

6 spring onions, finely chopped

juice of 1 lime or lemon

2 fl oz (65 ml) olive oil

3 tbsp chopped fresh coriander, plus more for garnishing

salt and pepper

1 Drain and rinse the black or red kidney beans. Place them in a large saucepan with half the water and garlic. Bring to the boil. Reduce the heat to low, cover and simmer until the beans are soft, about 1½ hours.

2 Drain and rinse the white beans. Put them in another saucepan with the remaining water and garlic. Bring to a boil, cover and simmer until soft, about 1 hour.

3 ▲ Purée the cooked haricot or white beans in a food processor or blender. Stir in the vinegar, chilli peppers and half the spring onions. Return to the saucepan and reheat gently.

4 Purée the other cooked beans. Return to the saucepan and stir in the lime or lemon juice, olive oil, coriander and the remaining spring onions. Reheat gently.

5 ▲ Season both soups with salt and pepper. To serve, place a ladleful of each puréed soup in each soup bowl, side by side. Swirl the two soups together with a cocktail stick. If liked, garnish with extra chopped fresh coriander.

Warming Autumn Soup

SERVES 4

1 oz (30 g) butter or margarine

2 small onions, finely chopped

1 lb (450 g) butternut squash or pumpkin, peeled, seeded and cubed

2 pt (1.25 litres) chicken stock

8 oz (225 g) potatoes, cubed

1 tsp paprika

4 fl oz (125 ml) whipping cream (optional)

salt and pepper

1½ tbsp chopped fresh chives, plus whole chives, for garnishing

1 Melt the butter or margarine in a large saucepan. Add the onions and cook until soft, about 5 minutes.

2 ▲ Add the squash or pumpkin, stock, potatoes and paprika. Bring to the boil. Reduce the heat to low, cover the pan and simmer until the vegetables are soft, about 35 minutes.

3 Pour the soup into a food processor or blender and process until smooth. Return the soup to the pan and stir in the cream, if using. Season with salt and pepper. Reheat gently.

4 ▲ Stir in the chopped chives just before serving. If liked, garnish each serving with a few whole chives.

Spicy Mixed Bean Soup (top), Warming Autumn Soup

Fried Cheddar and Chutney Sandwiches

SERVES 4

1½ oz (45 g) butter or margarine

3 large garlic cloves, crushed

3 fl oz (85 ml) homemade or bottled mango chutney

8 slices of white bread

8 oz (225 g) Cheddar cheese, grated

2 ▲ Spread the chutney on 4 slices of bread.

4 ▲ Brush both sides of each sandwich with the garlic butter.

5 Fry the sandwiches in a hot frying pan over a medium heat until golden brown, about 2 minutes on each side. Serve immediately.

1 ▲ Melt the butter or margarine in a small saucepan. Add the garlic and cook until softened but not brown, about 2 minutes, stirring. Remove from the heat.

3 ▲ Divide the cheese among the 4 bread slices, spreading it evenly. Top with the remaining bread slices.

> ~ **COOK'S TIP** ~
>
> Well-aged mature cheddar cheese works best in combination with the strong flavours of the chutney and garlic.

Tuna and Tomato Rolls

SERVES 4

2 × 7 oz (200 g) cans tuna fish, drained

2 tbsp finely chopped black olives

2 fl oz (65 ml) finely chopped drained sun-dried tomatoes preserved in oil

3 spring onions, finely chopped

4 round white bread rolls, split open

1 handful rocket or small lettuce leaves

FOR THE DRESSING

1½ tbsp red wine vinegar

5 tbsp olive oil

3 tbsp chopped fresh basil

salt and pepper

1 ▼ For the dressing, combine the vinegar and oil in a mixing bowl. Whisk until an emulsion is formed. Stir in the basil. Season with salt and pepper.

2 Add the tuna, olives, sun-dried tomatoes and spring onions and stir.

3 ▲ Divide the tuna mixture among the rolls. Top with the rocket or lettuce leaves and replace the tops of the rolls, pressing them on firmly.

Fried Cheddar and Chutney Sandwiches (top), Tuna and Tomato Rolls

Roast Beef and Horseradish Open Sandwiches

Serves 4

4 slices of pumpernickel or rye bread

12 oz (350 g) roast beef, thinly sliced

salt and pepper

4 tbsp mayonnaise

1½ tbsp prepared horseradish

2 small tomatoes, seeded and chopped

2–2 tbsp finely chopped pickled gherkin

fresh dill sprigs, for garnishing

1 ▲ Lay the slices of pumpernickel or rye bread on a flat surface. Divide the slices of roast beef between the bread, folding the slices in half, if large. Season with salt and pepper.

2 In a small bowl, combine the mayonnaise and horseradish. Stir in the tomatoes and pickled gherkin.

3 ▲ Spoon the horseradish mayonnaise onto the beef. Garnish with dill sprigs and serve.

Roast Pork and Coleslaw Rolls

Serves 6

6 fl oz (175 ml) mayonnaise

2 tbsp tomato ketchup

¼–½ tsp cayenne pepper

1 tbsp light brown sugar

1 lb (450 g) roast pork, thinly sliced

1 lb (450 g) green or white cabbage, cut into wedges

2 carrots, finely grated

1 small green pepper, seeded and diced

½ small red onion, finely chopped

12 small round white bread rolls, split open

1 ▲ In a bowl, combine the mayonnaise, ketchup, cayenne and brown sugar. Stir well.

2 Stack the slices of roast pork. With a sharp knife, cut them into matchstick strips.

3 Remove the cores from the cabbage wedges. Lay them on a chopping board and cut into fine strips across the leaves.

4 ▲ Add the pork, cabbage, carrots, green pepper and red onion to the mayonnaise mixture. Toss to mix.

5 ▲ Fill the split bread rolls with the pork and coleslaw mixure.

~ **VARIATIONS** ~

Instead of roast pork, substitute cooked ham or turkey, and prepare as above. As an alternative, try tuna in place of meat.

Roast Beef and Horseradish Open Sandwiches (top), Roast Pork and Coleslaw Rolls

Baked Cheeses with Red Pepper Sauce

SERVES 4

12 oz (350 g) log of goat cheese, cut into 12 equal slices

4 oz (115 g) dry breadcrumbs

1 tbsp chopped fresh parsley

1½ oz (45 g) Parmesan cheese, freshly grated

2 eggs, beaten

fresh parsley, for garnishing

FOR THE SAUCE

4 tbsp olive oil

4 garlic cloves, chopped

2 red peppers, seeded and chopped

1 tsp fresh thyme leaves

2 tsp tomato purée

salt and pepper

1 Preheat a 450°F/230°C/Gas 8 oven.

2 ▼ For the sauce, heat the olive oil in a saucepan. Add the garlic, red peppers and thyme and cook until the vegetables are soft, about 10 minutes, stirring frequently.

3 Pour the pepper mixture into a food processor or blender and purée. Return the puréed mixture to the saucepan. Stir in the tomato purée and salt and pepper to taste. Set aside.

4 ▲ Place each slice of cheese between two pieces of greaseproof paper. With the flat side of a large knife, flatten the cheese slightly.

5 ▲ In a small bowl, combine the breadcrumbs, parsley and Parmesan cheese. Pour the mixture onto a plate.

6 ▲ Dip the cheese rounds in the beaten egg, then in the breadcrumb mixture, coating well on all sides. Place on an ungreased baking tray.

7 Bake the cheese until golden, about 5 minutes. Meanwhile, gently reheat the sauce.

8 To serve, spoon some sauce on 4 heated plates. Place the baked cheese slices on top and garnish with parsley. Pass the remaining sauce.

Cheese and Dill Soufflés

SERVES 6

2 tbsp grated Parmesan cheese
2 oz (55 g) butter or margarine
1½ oz (45 g) plain flour
10 fl oz (300 ml) milk
4 oz (115 g) mature Cheddar cheese, grated
3 eggs, separated
2 tbsp chopped fresh dill
salt and pepper

1 Preheat a 400°F/200°C/Gas 6 oven. Butter 6 ramekins, and dust with the Parmesan cheese.

2 ▲ Melt the butter or margarine in a saucepan. Add the flour and cook 2 minutes, stirring. Stir in the milk. Bring to a boil, stirring constantly, and simmer until thickened, about 5 minutes. Remove from the heat and let cool about 10 minutes.

3 ▲ Stir the cheese, egg yolks and dill into the sauce. Season with salt and pepper. Transfer to a bowl.

4 In a clean mixing bowl, beat the egg whites with ⅛ teaspoon salt until stiff peaks form.

5 ▲ Stir one-quarter of the egg whites into the cheese sauce mixture to lighten it. Fold in the remaining egg whites.

6 ▲ Divide the mixture evenly between the prepared dishes. Bake until the soufflés are puffed and golden, 15–20 minutes. Serve immediately.

Cheesy Twists with Fruit Sauce

MAKES 12

6 large sheets of frozen filo pastry, thawed

4 oz (115 g) butter or margarine, melted

8 oz (225 g) Brie cheese, finely diced

FOR THE SAUCE

3 oz (85 g) cranberries or redcurrants

2 tbsp light brown sugar

1 For the sauce, combine the cranberries or redcurrants and sugar in a small saucepan with just enough water to cover. Bring to the boil and simmer until the fruit 'pop', about 3 minutes, stirring.

2 ▼ Pour the fruit mixture into a blender or food processor and process until finely chopped. Press it through a fine-mesh nylon sieve into a bowl. Taste and add more sugar if needed. Set aside.

3 Preheat a 450°F/230°C/Gas 8 oven.

4 ▲ To make the cheesy twists, cut the filo pastry into 36 × 5 in (13 cm) squares. Lay one pastry square on a flat surface and brush with some of the butter or margarine. Lay a second pastry square on top, placing it so the corners are not on top of each other. Brush with butter. Lay a third pastry square on top, again placing it so the corners are not on top of the others, thus forming a 12-pointed star.

5 Put a heaped tablespoon of the diced cheese in the centre of each pastry star.

6 ▲ Bring the points of each pastry star up over the cheese and twist to close securely. Fold back the tips of the points.

7 Arrange the twists on a baking tray. Bake until the pastry is crisp and golden brown, 10–15 minutes.

8 Meanwhile, gently reheat the fruit sauce. Serve the cheese twists hot with the sauce.

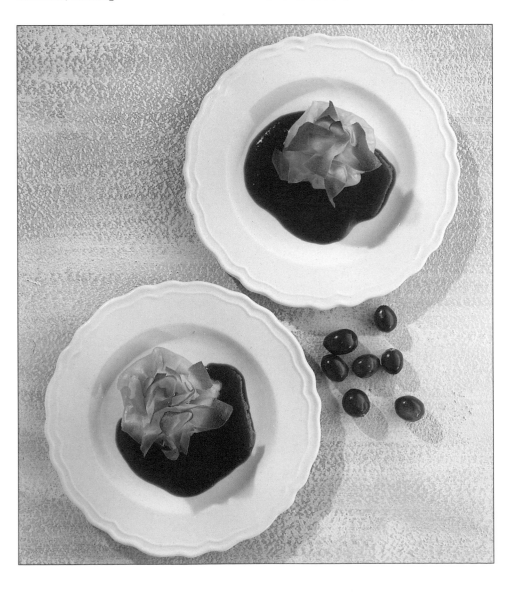

Spicy Bean Snacks

SERVES 8

2 tbsp vegetable oil
2 onions, chopped
2 garlic cloves, chopped
3 chilli peppers, seeded and chopped
1½ tbsp mild chilli powder
1 × 16 oz (450 g) can red kidney beans, drained and liquid reserved
3 tbsp chopped fresh coriander
nacho chips (fried tortilla rounds) or tortilla chips, for serving
8 oz (225 g) Cheddar cheese, grated
3 oz (85 g) stoned black olives, thinly sliced
fresh coriander sprigs, for garnishing

1 Preheat a 425°F/220°C/Gas 7 oven.

2 ▼ Heat the oil in a frying pan. Add the onions, garlic and chilli peppers and cook until soft, about 5 minutes. Add the chilli powder and cook 1 minute more.

~ **VARIATION** ~

To serve as a bean dip, stir in the cheese and olives. Transfer the bean mixture to a round earthenware dish. Bake until the cheese melts and browns slightly, 10–15 minutes. Garnish with coriander, and serve with tortilla chips for dipping.

3 ▲ Stir the beans into the onion mixture with 4 fl oz (125 ml) of the reserved can liquid. Cook until thickened, about 10 minutes, mashing the beans with a fork from time to time. Remove the pan from the heat and stir in the chopped coriander.

4 ▼ Put a little of the bean mixture on each nacho chip. Top each nacho with a little cheese and a slice of olive. Arrange on a baking tray.

5 Bake until the cheese has melted and is beginning to brown, 5–10 minutes. Serve immediately. Garnish with coriander, if liked.

Pancakes with Soured Cream and Salmon

MAKES 25

8 oz (225 g) salmon fillet, skinned

juice of 1 lime or lemon

2 fl oz (65 ml) extra-virgin olive oil

pinch salt

3 tbsp chopped fresh dill

5 fl oz (150 ml) soured cream

¼ avocado, peeled and diced

3 tbsp chopped fresh chives

fresh dill sprigs, for garnishing

FOR THE PANCAKES

3 oz (85 g) buckwheat flour

2 tsp caster sugar

1 egg

4 fl oz (125 ml) milk

1 oz (30 g) butter or margarine, melted

½ tsp cream of tartar

¼ tsp bicarbonate of soda

1 tbsp water

1 ▲ With a long, sharp knife, slice the salmon as thinly as possible. Place the slices, in one layer, in a large non-metallic dish.

~ **COOK'S TIP** ~

For easy entertaining, make the pancakes early in the day and store, covered. To serve, arrange them on a baking tray, and reheat in a preheated 400°F/200°C/Gas 6 oven until hot, 3–4 minutes.

2 ▲ In a small bowl, combine the lime juice, olive oil, salt and chopped dill. Pour the mixture over the salmon. Cover tightly and refrigerate several hours or overnight.

3 ▲ For the pancakes, combine the buckwheat flour and sugar in a mixing bowl. Set aside.

4 ▲ In a small bowl, beat together the egg, milk and butter or margarine. Gradually stir the egg mixture into the flour mixture. Stir in the cream of tartar, bicarbonate of soda and water.

5 ▲ Cover the bowl and let the batter stand 1 hour.

6 With a sharp knife, cut the marinated salmon in thin strips.

7 ▲ To cook the pancakes, heat a heavy non-stick frying pan. Using a large spoon, drop the batter into the pan to make small pancakes about 2 in (5 cm) in diameter. When bubbles appear on the surface, turn over. Cook until the other side is golden brown, 1–2 minutes longer. Transfer the pancakes to a plate and continue until all the batter is used.

8 ▲ To serve, place a teaspoon of soured cream on each pancake and top with the marinated salmon. Sprinkle with the diced avocado and chives and garnish with dill sprigs.

Mini Tomato Pastry 'Pizzas'

SERVES 6

4 large or 8 small sheets of frozen filo pastry, thawed
2 fl oz (65 ml) olive oil
1 lb (450 g) tomatoes, peeled, seeded and diced
2 oz (55 g) Parmesan cheese, grated
4 oz (115 g) feta cheese, crumbled
9 black olives, stoned and halved
¼ tsp dried oregano
½ tsp fresh thyme leaves, or ⅛ tsp dried thyme
salt and pepper
fresh thyme or basil, for garnishing

1 Preheat a 350°F/180°C/Gas 4 oven. Grease 2 baking trays.

2 ▲ Stack the filo sheets. With a sharp knife, cut into 24 × 6 in (15 cm) rounds, using a small plate as a guide.

3 ▲ Lay 3 filo rounds on each baking tray. Brush the rounds lightly with olive oil. Lay another pastry round on top of each oiled round and brush it with oil. Continue layering the pastry rounds, oiling each one, to make 6 stacks of 4 rounds each.

4 Bake the filo bases until they are crisp and golden brown, about 5 minutes.

5 ▲ In a bowl, combine the tomatoes, cheeses, olives and herbs. Mix well. Season with salt and pepper.

6 ▲ Spoon the tomato mixture on top of the filo pastry bases, leaving the edges bare. Return to the oven to bake until heated through, about 5 minutes.

7 Serve hot, garnished with fresh herb sprigs.

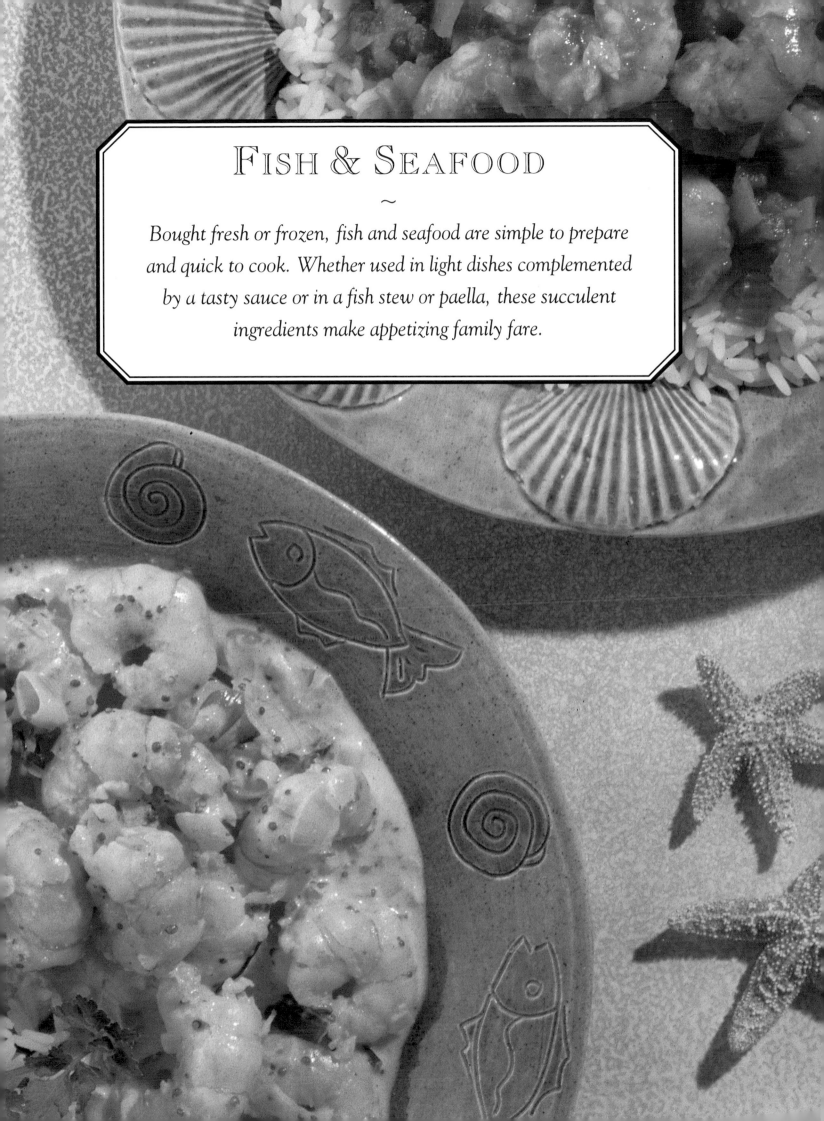

FISH & SEAFOOD

~

Bought fresh or frozen, fish and seafood are simple to prepare and quick to cook. Whether used in light dishes complemented by a tasty sauce or in a fish stew or paella, these succulent ingredients make appetizing family fare.

Paella

SERVES 6

4 tbsp olive oil

10 oz (300 g) short-grain rice

1 large onion, chopped

1 red pepper, seeded and chopped

12 oz (350 g) squid, cleaned and cut into rings (optional)

18 fl oz (500 ml) fish or chicken stock

4 fl oz (125 ml) dry white wine

½ tsp saffron strands

1 large garlic clove, crushed

8 fl oz (250 ml) canned chopped tomatoes

1 bay leaf

¼ tsp finely grated lemon rind

4 oz (115 g) chorizo or other spicy cooked sausage, cut into ¼ in (5 mm) slices

salt and pepper

7 oz (200 g) fresh or frozen green peas

12 oz (350 g) monkfish, skinned and cut into 1 in (2.5 cm) pieces

24 mussels, well scrubbed

12 raw or cooked prawns, peeled and deveined

1 ▼ Heat the oil in a large frying pan or paella pan. Add the rice and cook over a medium-high heat until it begins to colour, stirring frequently.

2 ▲ Stir in the onion and pepper and cook 2–3 minutes longer.

3 ▲ Add the squid, if using, and cook, stirring occasionally, until it is lightly browned.

4 Stir in the stock, wine, saffron, and garlic. Bring to the boil.

5 ▲ Add the tomatoes, bay leaf, lemon rind, and sausage. Season with salt and pepper. Return to the boil, then reduce the heat. Cover and simmer until the rice has absorbed most of the liquid, about 15 minutes.

6 ▲ Add the peas, monkfish and mussels to the rice. Push the mussels down into the rice.

7 ▲ Gently stir in the prawns. Cover and continue cooking until the mussels have opened and the rice is tender, about 5 minutes. Raw prawns should have turned bright pink.

8 Taste and adjust the seasoning. Serve immediately in a heated serving dish or from the paella pan, if using.

~ COOK'S TIP ~

This recipe can be doubled to feed a crowd. Be sure to use a larger pan, such as a wide shallow flameproof casserole. The final simmering, after the pan has been covered (step 5), can be done in a preheated 375°F/190°C/Gas 5 oven. If using a paella pan, cover with foil.

Spicy Tomato Prawns

SERVES 4

2 oz (55 g) butter or margarine

3 garlic cloves, crushed

1 large onion, finely chopped

1 green pepper, seeded and diced

2 sticks celery, chopped

16 fl oz (450 ml) canned chopped
  tomatoes

1 tsp sugar

2 tsp salt

1 bay leaf

1½ tsp fresh thyme leaves, or ½ tsp
  dried thyme

¼ tsp cayenne pepper

2 lb (900 g) raw prawns, peeled and
  deveined, or cooked peeled prawns

½ tsp grated lemon rind

2 tbsp fresh lemon juice

pepper

1 Heat the butter or margarine in a
flameproof casserole. Add the garlic,
onion, pepper and celery and cook
until softened, about 5 minutes.

2 ▲ Add the tomatoes, sugar, salt,
bay leaf, thyme and cayenne. Bring to
the boil. Reduce the heat and simmer
10 minutes.

3 ▲ Stir in the prawns, lemon rind
and juice and pepper to taste. Cover
and simmer until raw prawns turn
pink, about 5 minutes, or until cooked
prawns are hot, about 2 minutes.

4 Serve immediately on a bed of
freshly cooked rice.

Prawns in Creamy Mustard Sauce

SERVES 4

2 oz (55 g) butter or margarine

2 lb (900 g) raw prawns, peeled and
  deveined, or cooked peeled prawns

1 small onion, finely chopped

4 spring onions, cut diagonally in ⅛ in
  (3 mm) lengths

2 tbsp fresh lemon juice

4 fl oz (125 ml) dry white wine

4 fl oz (125 ml) whipping cream

2 tbsp whole-grain mustard

salt and pepper

1 Melt half the butter or margarine in
a frying pan over high heat. Add raw
prawns, if using, and cook until they
turn pink and opaque, about 2
minutes, stirring constantly. Remove
with a slotted spoon and set aside.

2 Melt the remaining butter or
margarine in the frying pan. Add the
onion and spring onions and cook
until softened, 3–4 minutes, stirring
frequently.

3 ▲ Stir in the lemon juice and
wine. Bring to the boil, scraping the
bottom of the pan with a wooden
spoon to mix in the cooking juices.

4 ▲ Add the cream. Simmer until
the mixture thickens, 3–4 minutes,
stirring frequently. Stir in the
mustard.

5 Return the fried prawns to the pan
and reheat briefly. Add cooked
prawns at this stage and heat through,
about 2 minutes. Season with salt and
pepper and serve.

Spicy Tomato Prawns (top), Prawns in Creamy Mustard Sauce

Crab Cakes

SERVES 3 OR 6

1 lb (450 g) fresh white crab meat

1 egg, well beaten

1 tsp Dijon mustard

2 tsp prepared horseradish

2 tsp Worcestershire sauce

8 spring onions, finely chopped

3 tbsp chopped fresh parsley

3 oz (85 g) fresh breadcrumbs

salt and pepper

1 tbsp whipping cream (optional)

2 oz (55 g) dry breadcrumbs

1½ oz (45 g) butter or margarine

lemon wedges, for serving

1 In a mixing bowl, combine the crab meat, egg, mustard, horseradish, Worcestershire sauce, spring onions, parsley, fresh breadcrumbs and seasoning. Mix gently, leaving the pieces of crab meat as large as possible. If the mixture is too dry to hold together, add the cream.

2 ▲ Divide the crab mixture into 6 portions and shape.

3 ▲ Put the dry breadcrumbs on a plate. Coat the crab cakes on both sides with the breadcrumbs.

4 Melt the butter or margarine in a frying pan. Fry the crab cakes until golden, about 3 minutes on each side. Add more fat if necessary.

5 Serve 1 or 2 per person, with lemon wedges.

Baked Stuffed Crab

SERVES 4

4 freshly cooked crabs

1 celery stick, diced

1 spring onion, finely chopped

1 small fresh green chilli pepper, seeded and finely chopped

3 fl oz (85 ml) mayonnaise

2 tbsp fresh lemon juice

1 tbsp chopped fresh chives

salt and pepper

1 oz (30 g) fresh breadcrumbs

2 oz (55 g) Cheddar cheese, grated

1 oz (30 g) butter or margarine, melted

parsley sprigs, for garnishing

1 Preheat a 375°F/190°C/Gas 5 oven.

2 ▼ Pull the claws and legs from each crab. Separate the body from the shell. Scoop out the meat from the shell. Discard the feathery gills and the intestines; remove the meat and coral from the body. Crack the claws and remove the meat.

3 Scrub the shells. Cut into the seam on the underside with scissors. The inner part of the shell should break off cleanly along the seam, enlarging the opening. Rinse the shells and dry them well.

4 In a bowl, combine the crab meat, celery, spring onion, chilli pepper, mayonnaise, lemon juice and chives. Season with salt and pepper to taste and mix well.

5 In another bowl, toss together the breadcrumbs, cheese, and melted butter or margarine.

6 ▲ Pile the crab mixture into the shells. Sprinkle with the cheese mixture. Bake until golden brown, about 20 minutes. Serve hot, garnished with parsley sprigs.

Crab Cakes (top), Baked Stuffed Crab

Halibut with Fruity Sauce

SERVES 4

4 halibut steaks (about 1½ lb/700 g)

1 oz (30 g) butter or margarine, melted

salt and pepper

fresh mint sprigs, for garnishing

FOR THE SAUCE

2½ oz (70 g) fresh pineapple, finely diced

2 tbsp diced red pepper

1 tbsp finely chopped red onion

finely grated rind of 1 lemon

1 tbsp lemon juice

1 tsp honey

2 tbsp chopped fresh mint

1 For the sauce, combine the pineapple, red pepper, red onion, lemon rind and juice and honey in a small bowl. Stir to mix. Cover with cling film and refrigerate for 30 minutes.

2 Preheat the grill.

3 ▲ Brush the halibut with butter or margarine and sprinkle with salt and pepper. Arrange on the rack in the grill pan, buttered-side up.

4 Grill the steaks about 3 in (8 cm) from the heat, turning once and brushing with the remaining butter or margarine, about 5 minutes on each side. Transfer to warmed serving plates.

5 ▲ Stir the chopped mint into the sauce. Garnish the halibut with mint sprigs and serve with the sauce.

Thick and Creamy Fish Stew

SERVES 4

3 thick-cut rashers of bacon, cut into small pieces

1 large onion, chopped

2 large potatoes, cut in ¾ in (2 cm) cubes (about 1½ lb/700 g)

salt and pepper

1¾ pt (1 litre) fish stock

1 lb (450 g) skinless haddock or cod fillet, cut into 1 in (2.5 cm) cubes

2 tbsp chopped fresh parsley

1 tbsp chopped fresh chives

8 fl oz (250 ml) whipping cream or milk

1 Fry the bacon in a deep saucepan until the fat is rendered. Add the onion and potatoes and cook over a low heat, without browning, about 10 minutes. Season to taste with salt and pepper.

2 ▲ Pour off excess fat from the pan. Add the fish stock to the pan and bring to the boil. Simmer until the vegetables are tender, 15–20 minutes.

3 ▲ Stir in the cubes of fish, the parsley and chives. Simmer until the fish is just cooked, 3–4 minutes.

4 Stir the cream or milk into the chowder and reheat gently. Season to taste and serve immediately.

Halibut with Fruity Sauce (top), Thick and Creamy Fish Stew

Fish with Orange and Caper Sauce

SERVES 4

2 fl oz (65 ml) fresh orange juice

1 tsp soy sauce

2 tbsp olive oil

4 × 8 oz (225 g) swordfish or other firm, white fish steaks

salt and pepper

1½ oz (45 g) cold butter or margarine, cut into pieces

2 tbsp capers in vinegar

1 tbsp chopped fresh parsley

1 In a small bowl, combine the orange juice, soy sauce and 1 tablespoon of the olive oil. Whisk to mix.

2 Lay the fish steaks in a shallow baking dish. Pour the orange-soy mixture over them and sprinkle with salt and pepper.

3 Heat the remaining tablespoon of olive oil in a heavy frying pan over a medium-high heat.

4 ▲ Drain the fish steaks, reserving the marinade. Add the steaks to the frying pan and cook until the fish flakes easily when tested with a fork, 3–4 minutes on each side, basting occasionally with the reserved marinade. Transfer the fish steaks to a warmed serving platter.

5 ▲ Pour the reserved marinade into the pan and cook 1 minute, stirring to mix in the cooking juices. Add the butter or margarine, capers with their vinegar, and parsley. Cook until the butter has melted and the sauce is slightly syrupy.

6 Pour the sauce over the fish steaks and serve immediately.

Tuna with Oriental Dressing

SERVES 6

6 tuna steaks (about 2 lb/900 g)

FOR THE DRESSING

1 in (2.5 cm) piece of fresh root ginger, peeled and finely grated

2 spring onions, thinly sliced

2 tbsp chopped fresh chives

grated rind and juice of 1 lime or lemon

2 tbsp dry sherry

1 tbsp soy sauce

4 fl oz (125 ml) olive oil

salt and pepper

1 ▲ For the dressing, combine the ginger, spring onions, chives, lime rind and juice, sherry and soy sauce. Add the olive oil and whisk to mix. Season and set aside.

2 Preheat the grill. Sprinkle the tuna steaks with salt and pepper.

3 ▼ Arrange the tuna steaks on the rack in the grill pan. Grill about 3 in (8 cm) from the heat for about 5 minutes on each side, until the fish flakes easily when tested with a fork.

4 Arrange the cooked fish on a warmed serving platter or individual plates. Spoon the dressing over the fish and serve.

Fish with Orange and Caper Sauce (top), Tuna with Oriental Dressing

Crispy Cod Steaks with Tomato Sauce

SERVES 4

3 tbsp cornmeal, or polenta

½ tsp salt

¼ tsp hot chilli powder

4 cod steaks, each 1 in (2.5 cm) thick (about 1½ lb/700 g)

2 tbsp vegetable oil

fresh basil sprigs, for garnishing

FOR THE TOMATO SAUCE

2 tbsp olive oil

1 shallot, or ½ small onion, finely chopped

1 garlic clove, crushed

1 lb (450 g) ripe tomatoes, chopped, or 1 16 oz (450 g) can chopped tomatoes

⅛ tsp sugar

2 fl oz (65 ml) dry white wine

2 tbsp chopped fresh basil, or ½ tsp dried basil

salt and pepper

1 For the sauce, heat the oil in a saucepan. Add the shallot or onion and the garlic and cook until soft, about 5 minutes. Stir in the tomatoes, sugar, wine and basil. Bring to a boil. Simmer until thickened, 10–15 minutes.

2 ▲ Work the sauce through a vegetable mill or sieve until smooth. Return it to the pan. Season with salt and pepper. Set aside.

3 ▲ Combine the cornmeal or polenta, salt and chilli powder on a sheet of greaseproof paper.

4 ▲ Rinse the cod steaks, then dip them on both sides into the cornmeal mixture, patting gently until evenly coated.

5 ▲ Heat the oil in a large frying pan. Add the cod steaks and cook until golden brown and the flesh will flake easily when tested with a fork, about 5 minutes on each side. Cook in batches if necessary. Meanwhile, reheat the tomato sauce.

6 Garnish the cod steaks with basil sprigs and serve with the tomato sauce.

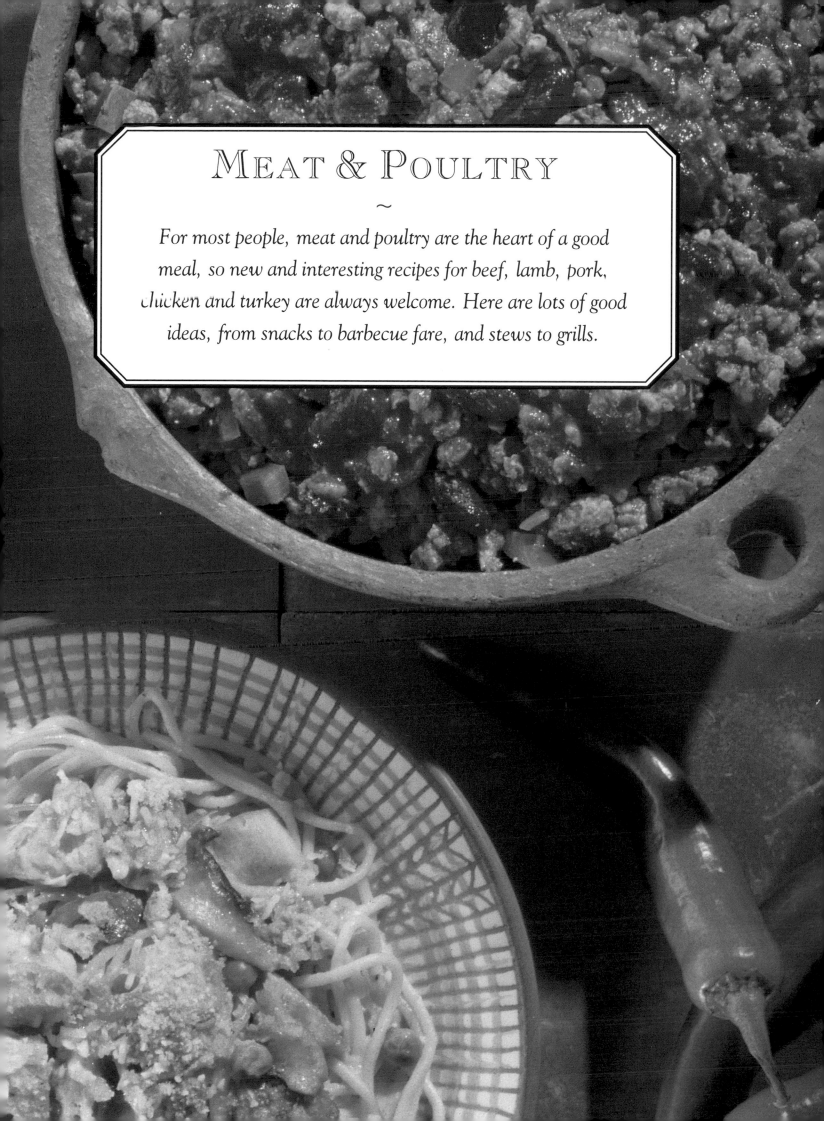

MEAT & POULTRY

~

For most people, meat and poultry are the heart of a good meal, so new and interesting recipes for beef, lamb, pork, chicken and turkey are always welcome. Here are lots of good ideas, from snacks to barbecue fare, and stews to grills.

Layered Meat and Fruit Loaf

SERVES 6

1½ lb (700 g) minced beef

8 oz (225 g) minced pork

2 eggs, lightly beaten

2 oz (55 g) fresh breadcrumbs

¼ tsp ground cinnamon

salt and pepper

FOR THE STUFFING

½ oz (15 g) butter or margarine

1 small onion, chopped

1½ oz (45 g) chopped dried figs

1½ oz (45 g) chopped dried apricots

1½ oz (45 g) sultanas

1 oz (30 g) pine kernels

4 fl oz (125 ml) dry white wine

2 tbsp chopped fresh parsley

1 Preheat a 350°F/180°C/Gas 4 oven.

2 ▼ For the stuffing, melt the butter or margarine in a small frying pan. Add the onion and cook until softened, about 5 minutes. Stir in the figs, apricots, raisins, pine kernels and wine. Bring to the boil and boil to evaporate the liquid, about 5 minutes. Remove from the heat and stir in the parsley. Set aside.

3 In a bowl, mix together the beef, pork, eggs, breadcrumbs, cinnamon and a little salt and pepper.

4 ▲ Press half of the meat mixture in a 9 × 5 in (23 × 13 cm) loaf tin. Spoon the stuffing over the meat. Spread the remaining meat mixture on top and press down gently.

5 Cover the tin with foil. Bake 1¼ hours. Pour off any excess fat from the tin. Let the meat loaf cool slightly before serving.

Steak with Spicy Mushroom Sauce

SERVES 4

2½ oz (70 g) butter or margarine

1 lb (450 g) mushrooms, quartered

1 shallot or ½ small onion, finely chopped

3 tbsp chopped fresh parsley

salt and pepper

4 sirloin steaks, each about 1 in (2.5 cm) thick

1 onion, thinly sliced

⅛ tsp crushed dried chilli pepper

⅛ tsp cayenne pepper

dash of chilli sauce

2 tsp Worcestershire sauce

2 tsp sugar

5 fl oz (150 ml) brandy

8 fl oz (250 ml) beef stock

1 ▼ Melt 1 oz (30 g) of the butter or margarine in a frying pan. Add the mushrooms and shallot and cook until softened, about 5 minutes. Drain off the excess liquid. Sprinkle the mushrooms with the parsley and a little salt and pepper. Set aside.

2 Preheat the grill. Sprinkle the steaks with salt and pepper and arrange them on the rack in the grill pan. Set aside.

3 Melt the remaining butter or margarine in a saucepan. Add the onion and cook until softened, about 5 minutes. Stir in the dried chilli pepper, cayenne, chilli sauce, Worcestershire sauce, sugar and brandy. Bring to the boil and boil until the sauce is reduced by half.

4 Meanwhile, grill the steaks about 3 in (8 cm) from the heat, 5 minutes on each side for medium-rare, 8 minutes on each side for medium.

5 While the steaks are cooking, add the stock to the sauce and boil again to reduce by half. Season to taste with salt and pepper. Stir in the cooked mushrooms.

6 Transfer the steaks to heated plates and spoon the sauce on top.

Layered Meat and Fruit Loaf (top), Steak with Spicy Mushroom Sauce

Boiled Beef Platter

SERVES 6

2–2½ lb (about 1 kg) salted brisket

1 tsp black peppercorns

2 bay leaves

1 small swede, about 1 lb (450 g), cut into pieces

8 button onions

8 small red potatoes

3 carrots, cut into sticks

1 small head of green cabbage, cut into 6 wedges

FOR THE SAUCE

3 fl oz (85 ml) red wine vinegar

2 oz (55 g) sugar

1 tbsp mustard powder

about 2 oz (55 g) butter or margarine

salt and pepper

1 Put the brisket in a large pan. Add the peppercorns and bay leaves and cover with water. Bring to the boil. Reduce the heat and simmer until the beef is almost tender, about 2 hours.

2 ▼ Add the swede, onions, potatoes and carrots. Bring the liquid back to the boil, then reduce the heat and cover the pan. Simmer 10 minutes.

3 Add the cabbage wedges. Cover and cook 15 minutes longer.

4 With a slotted spoon, remove the meat and vegetables from the pan and keep them hot. Reserve 12 fl oz (350 ml) of the cooking liquid.

5 ▲ For the sauce, combine the reserved cooking liquid, vinegar, sugar and mustard in a small saucepan. Bring to the boil, then reduce the heat and simmer until thickened, about 5 minutes. Remove the pan from the heat and swirl in the butter or margarine. Season to taste with salt and pepper.

6 Slice the beef and arrange with the vegetables on a warmed platter. Serve with the sauce in a sauceboat.

Steak Sandwiches with Onions

SERVES 3

3 pieces thinly cut rump steak (about 1 lb/450 g)

salt and pepper

1 oz (30 g) butter or margarine

2 tbsp vegetable oil

1 large onion, thinly sliced into rings

1 long French stick, split in half lengthwise, and cut into 3 sections

Dijon mustard, for serving

1 Sprinkle the steaks generously with salt and pepper.

2 ▲ Heat the butter or margarine and half the oil in a frying pan. Add the onion and cook until browned and crispy, about 8 minutes. Remove the onion with a slotted spoon and drain on kitchen paper. Add the remaining oil to the pan.

3 ▼ Add the steaks to the frying pan and cook until well browned, about 3 minutes, turning once.

4 Divide the steak and onions among the bottom halves of the bread sections, and put on the tops. Serve on warmed plates with mustard.

Boiled Beef Platter (top), Steak Sandwiches with Onions

Lamb Chops with Basil Sauce

SERVES 4

small bunch of fresh basil leaves

1 oz (30 g) pine kernels

2 garlic cloves

1 oz (30 g) Parmesan cheese, diced

4 fl oz (125 ml) extra-virgin olive oil

salt and pepper

4 lamb sirloin or chump chops, about
     8 oz (225 g) each

fresh basil sprigs, for garnishing

1 In a food processor or blender,
combine the basil, pine kernels, garlic
and Parmesan cheese. Process until
the ingredients are finely chopped.
Gradually pour in the olive oil in a
thin stream. Season to taste with salt
and pepper. The sauce should be thin
and creamy. Alternatively, use a
mortar and pestle to make the sauce.

2 ▼ Put the lamb chops in a shallow
dish that will hold them comfortably
side by side. Pour the basil sauce over
the chops. Turn to coat on both sides.
Let marinate 1 hour.

3 Preheat the grill. Brush the rack in
the grill pan with olive oil.

4 ▲ Transfer the chops to the grill
rack. Grill about 3 in (8 cm) from the
heat until well browned and cooked to
taste, about 15 minutes, turning once.
Serve garnished with fresh basil sprigs.

Lamb and Bean Stew

SERVES 6

9 oz (250 g) dried red kidney beans,
     soaked overnight and drained

2 tbsp vegetable oil

2 lb (900 g) lean boned lamb, cut into
     1½ in (3 cm) cubes

1 large onion, chopped

1 bay leaf

1¼ pt (750 ml) chicken stock

1 garlic clove, crushed

salt and pepper

1 Put the beans in a large pot. Cover
with fresh water, bring to the boil and
boil 10 minutes. Reduce the heat and
simmer 30 minutes, then drain.

2 Meanwhile, heat the oil in another
large pot. Add the lamb cubes and fry
until browned all over. Remove the
lamb with a slotted spoon and reserve
until needed.

3 ▼ Add the onion to the hot oil
and cook until softened, about 5
minutes.

4 ▲ Return the lamb cubes to the
pot and add the drained beans, bay
leaf, stock, garlic and salt and pepper
to taste. Bring to the boil. Reduce the
heat, cover and simmer 1¼ hours, or
until the lamb and beans are tender.

5 Discard the bay leaf and adjust the
seasoning before serving.

Lamb Chops with Basil Sauce (top), Lamb and Bean Stew

Spicy Pork on Tortilla Pancakes

SERVES 4

1 garlic clove, crushed
2 tbsp vegetable oil
3 fl oz (85 ml) fresh lime juice
3 tbsp Worcestershire sauce
⅛ tsp pepper
1¼ lb (575 g) pork cutlets, cut lengthwise into ⅜ in (1 cm) strips
1 large ripe avocado
4 tbsp finely chopped fresh coriander leaves
8 corn tortillas
1 onion, sliced
1 green pepper, seeded and sliced
black olives, for garnishing

FOR THE SALSA

8 oz (225 g) drained canned sweetcorn, or frozen sweetcorn, thawed
1 small red pepper, seeded and finely chopped
1 small red onion, thinly sliced
1 tsp honey
juice of 1 lime or lemon

1 ▼ In a medium bowl, combine the garlic, 1 tablespoon of the oil, the lime juice, Worcestershire sauce and pepper. Add the pork strips and toss to coat. Let marinate 10–20 minutes, stirring the strips at least once.

2 ▲ Meanwhile, combine all the ingredients for the salsa in a bowl and mix well. Set aside.

3 ▲ Cut the avocado in half and remove the stone. Scrape the flesh into a bowl and mash it with a fork. Stir in the chopped coriander.

4 ▲ Preheat the oven to 350°F/180°C/Gas 4. Wrap the corn tortillas in foil and heat them in the oven for 10 minutes.

5 ▲ Meanwhile, heat the remaining oil in a frying pan. Add the onion and green pepper slices and cook until softened, about 5 minutes.

6 ▲ Add the pork strips to the frying pan and fry briskly, turning occasionally, until cooked and browned, about 5 minutes.

7 ▲ To serve, place a spoonful of the avocado on each of the heated tortillas. Top with some of the pork mixture and a spoonful of the salsa. Garnish with an olive, and serve with more salsa, if wished.

Pork Chops with Sauerkraut

6 rashers of bacon, coarsely chopped

3 tbsp plain flour

salt and pepper

6 boned loin pork chops

2 tsp light brown sugar

1 garlic clove, crushed

1½ lb (700 g) sauerkraut, rinsed

1 tsp juniper berries

1 tsp black peppercorns

8 fl oz (250 ml) beer

8 fl oz (250 ml) chicken stock

1 Preheat a 350°F/180°C/Gas 4 oven.

2 ▼ In a frying pan, fry the bacon until just beginning to brown. With a slotted spoon, transfer the bacon to a casserole dish.

3 ▲ Season the flour with salt and pepper. Coat the pork chops with the seasoned flour, shaking off any excess. Brown the chops in the bacon fat, about 5 minutes on each side. Remove and drain on kitchen paper.

4 ▲ Add the brown sugar and garlic to the fat in the frying pan and cook, stirring, for 3 minutes. Add the sauerkraut, juniper berries and peppercorns.

5 ▲ Transfer the sauerkraut mixture to the casserole and mix with the bacon. Lay the pork chops on top. Pour the beer and chicken stock over the chops.

6 Place the casserole in the oven and cook until the chops are very tender, 45–55 minutes.

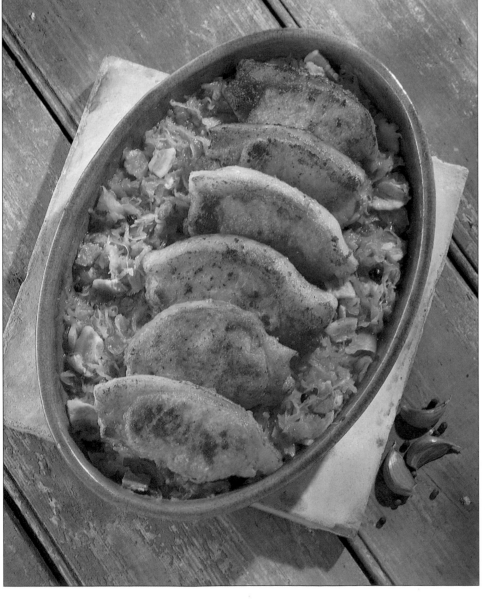

Barbecued Spareribs

SERVES 4

3 lb (1.35 kg) meaty pork spareribs

4 fl oz (125 ml) vegetable oil

½ tsp paprika

FOR THE SAUCE

3 oz (85 g) light brown sugar

2 tsp mustard powder

1 tsp salt

⅛ tsp pepper

½ tsp ground ginger

4 fl oz (125 ml) fresh tomatoes, skinned, cooked and sieved

4 fl oz (125 ml) orange juice

1 small onion, finely chopped

1 garlic clove, crushed

2 tbsp chopped fresh parsley

1 tbsp Worcestershire sauce

1 ▲ Preheat a 375°F/190°C/Gas 5 oven. Arrange the ribs in one layer in a roasting tin.

2 ▲ In a small bowl, combine the oil and paprika. Brush the mixture over the spareribs. Bake until the ribs are slightly crisp, 55–60 minutes.

3 ▼ Combine the sauce ingredients in a saucepan and bring to the boil. Simmer 5 minutes, stirring occasionally.

4 ▲ Pour off the fat from the roasting tin. Brush the ribs with half of the sauce and bake 20 minutes. Turn the ribs over and brush with the remaining sauce. Bake 20 minutes longer. Cut into sections for serving.

Baked Sausages and Beans with Crispy Topping

SERVES 6

12 oz (350 g) dried haricot or white beans, soaked overnight and drained

1 onion, stuck with 4 cloves

1½ oz (45 g) butter or margarine

1 lb (450 g) pork link sausages

1 lb (450 g) garlic sausage, cut into ½ in (1 cm) slices

4 oz (115 g) bacon, chopped

1 large onion, finely chopped

2 garlic cloves, crushed

1 × 16 oz (450 g) can chopped tomatoes

5 oz (140 g) can tomato purée

2 fl oz (65 ml) maple syrup

2 tbsp dark brown sugar

½ tsp mustard powder

¼ tsp salt

pepper

1 oz (30 g) fresh breadcrumbs

1 ▲ Put the beans in a saucepan and cover with fresh cold water. Add the clove-studded onion. Bring to the boil and boil until the beans are just tender, about 1 hour. Drain the beans. Discard the onion.

2 Preheat a 350°F/180°C/Gas 4 oven.

3 ▲ Melt half of the butter or margarine in a large flameproof casserole. Add the sausages, bacon, onion and garlic and fry until the bacon and sausages are well browned.

4 ▲ Stir in the beans, tomatoes, tomato purée, maple syrup, brown sugar, mustard, salt and pepper to taste. Bring to the boil.

5 ▲ Sprinkle the breadcrumbs over the surface and dot with the remaining butter or margarine.

6 Transfer the casserole to the oven and bake until most of liquid has been absorbed by the beans and the top is crisp, about 1 hour.

Jambalaya

2 tbsp vegetable oil

4 skinless boneless chicken breast
   halves, cut into chunks

1 lb (450 g) spicy cooked sausage, sliced

6 oz (170 g) smoked ham, cubed

1 large onion, chopped

2 celery sticks, chopped

2 green peppers, seeded and chopped

3 garlic cloves, crushed

8 fl oz (250 ml) canned chopped
   tomatoes

16 fl oz (450 ml) chicken stock

1 tsp cayenne pepper

1 sprig of fresh thyme, or ¼ tsp dried
   thyme

2 sprigs of flat-leaved parsley

1 bay leaf

10 oz (300 g) rice

salt and pepper

4 spring onions, finely chopped

1 ▼ Heat the oil in a large frying
pan. Add the chicken chunks and
sausage slices and cook until well
browned, about 5 minutes. Stir in the
ham cubes and cook 5 minutes longer.

2 Add the onion, celery, peppers,
garlic, tomatoes, stock, cayenne,
thyme, parsley and bay leaf to the
frying pan. Bring to the boil, stirring
well.

3 ▲ Stir in the rice, and add salt and
and pepper to taste. When the liquid
returns to the boil, reduce the heat
and cover the pan tightly. Simmer 10
minutes.

4 Remove the pan from the heat and,
without removing the lid, set aside for
20 minutes, to let the rice finish
cooking.

5 ▲ Discard the bay leaf. Scatter the
chopped spring onions on top of the
jambalaya just before serving.

Ham and Asparagus with Cheese Sauce

SERVES 4

24 asparagus spears

1½ oz (45 g) butter or margarine

3 tbsp plain flour

12 fl oz (350 ml) milk

4 oz (115 g) Gruyère or Cheddar cheese, grated

⅛ tsp grated nutmeg

salt and pepper

12 thin slices of cooked ham or Parma ham

1 Trim any tough stalk ends from the asparagus. Bring a wide shallow pan of salted water to the boil. Add the asparagus and simmer until barely tender, 5–7 minutes. Drain the asparagus in a colander, rinse with cold water and spread out on kitchen paper to dry.

2 Preheat the grill. Grease a 13 × 9 in (33 × 23 cm) baking dish.

3 Melt the butter or margarine in a saucepan. Add the flour and cook 2 minutes, stirring. Stir in the milk. Bring to the boil, stirring constantly, and simmer until thickened, about 5 minutes.

4 ▲ Add three-quarters of the cheese to the sauce. Season to taste with nutmeg, salt and pepper. Keep warm.

5 ▲ Wrap a pair of asparagus spears in each slice of ham. Arrange in the prepared baking dish, in one layer.

6 Pour the sauce over the ham and asparagus rolls and sprinkle the remaining cheese on top. Grill about 3 in (8 cm) from the heat until bubbling and golden brown, about 5 minutes. Serve hot.

Gammon Steaks with Raisin Sauce

SERVES 4

2 oz (55 g) raisins

8 fl oz (250 ml) warm water

½ tsp instant coffee

1 tsp cornflour

1½ oz (45 g) butter or margarine

4 gammon steaks, about 4 oz (115 g) each, trimmed of excess fat

2 tsp dark brown sugar

2 tsp cider vinegar

2 tsp soy sauce

~ **VARIATION** ~

For a richer sauce, substitute an equal quantity of chopped prunes for the raisins.

1 ▼ In a small bowl, soak the raisins in half of the water to plump them, about 10 minutes.

2 Stir the coffee and cornflour into the remaining water until smooth.

3 Melt the butter or margarine in a large frying pan. Add the gammon steaks and cook over a medium-low heat until lightly browned, about 5 minutes on each side.

4 ▲ Transfer the cooked steaks to a heated serving dish.

5 Drain the raisins and add them to the frying pan. Stir the coffee mixture to recombine it, then add to the pan with the sugar, vinegar and soy sauce. Bring to the boil and simmer until slightly thickened, about 3 minutes, stirring constantly.

6 Spoon the raisin sauce over the gammon steaks and serve.

Ham and Asparagus with Cheese Sauce (top), Gammon Steaks with Raisin Sauce

Hot Turkey Sandwich

SERVES 4

2 oz (55 g) butter or margarine

½ small onion, finely chopped

8 oz (225 g) button mushrooms, quartered

1¼ lb (575 g) roast turkey breast

4 thick slices of wholewheat bread

16 fl oz (450 ml) thick turkey gravy

parsley sprigs, for garnishing

1 Melt half the butter or margarine in a frying pan. Add the onion and cook until softened, about 5 minutes.

~ **VARIATION** ~

If preferred, the sandwich bread may be toasted and buttered.

2 Add the mushrooms and cook until the moisture they render has evaporated, about 5 minutes, stirring occasionally.

3 ▲ Meanwhile, skin the turkey breast, and carve into 4 thick slices.

4 In a saucepan, reheat the turkey gravy. Stir in the onion and mushroom mixture.

5 ▲ Spread the slices of bread with the remaining butter or margarine. Set a slice on each of 4 plates and top with the turkey slices. Pour the mushroom gravy over the turkey and serve hot, garnished with parsley.

Leftover Turkey Casserole

SERVES 6

4 fl oz (125 ml) vegetable oil

4 eggs

16 fl oz (450 ml) milk

4 oz (115 g) plain flour

salt and pepper

1½ lb (700 g) cooked turkey meat, cubed

4 fl oz (125 ml) thick plain yoghurt

3 oz (85 g) cornflakes, crushed

1 Preheat a 425°F/220°C/Gas 7 oven.

2 Pour the oil into a 13 × 9 in (33 × 23 cm) baking dish. Heat in the oven about 10 minutes.

3 Meanwhile, beat the eggs in a mixing bowl. Add the milk. Sift in the flour and add a little salt and pepper. Mix until the batter is smooth. Set aside.

4 ▲ Coat the turkey cubes in the yoghurt, then roll in the crushed cornflakes to coat all over.

5 ▲ Remove the baking dish from the oven and pour in the prepared batter. Arrange the turkey pieces on top. Return to the oven and bake until the batter is set and golden, 35–40 minutes. Serve hot.

Hot Turkey Sandwich (top), Leftover Turkey Casserole

Turkey Chilli

SERVES 8

2 tbsp vegetable oil

1 medium onion, halved and thinly sliced

1 green pepper, seeded and diced

3 garlic cloves, crushed

2 lb (900 g) minced turkey

2–3 tbsp mild chilli powder

1½ tsp ground cumin

1 tsp dried oregano

1 × 16 oz (450 g) can chopped tomatoes

2 tbsp tomato purée

8 fl oz (250 ml) chicken stock

1 × 16 oz (450 g) can red kidney beans, drained and rinsed

¼ tsp salt

1 Heat the oil in a large saucepan over a medium heat. Add the onion, green pepper and garlic and cook until softened, about 5 minutes, stirring frequently.

2 ▼ Add the turkey and cook until it is lightly browned, about 5 minutes longer, stirring to break up the meat.

3 ▼ Stir in the chilli powder, cumin and oregano. Add the tomatoes, tomato purée, chicken stock, kidney beans and salt, and stir well.

4 Bring to the boil, then reduce the heat and simmer 30 minutes, stirring occasionally. Serve the chilli with boiled rice.

Turkey and Pasta Bake

SERVES 4

2½ oz (70 g) butter or margarine

8 oz (225 g) mushrooms, thinly sliced

1 oz (30 g) plain flour

14 fl oz (400 ml) milk

16 fl oz (450 ml) chicken stock

2 fl oz (65 ml) dry white wine

10 oz (300 g) spaghetti

12 oz (350 g) chopped cooked turkey meat

5 oz (140 g) frozen peas, thawed and drained

2½ oz (70 g) Parmesan cheese, freshly grated

salt and pepper

1 oz (30 g) fine fresh breadcrumbs

1 Preheat a 375°F/190°C/Gas 5 oven. Grease a shallow 5 pt (3 litre) baking dish.

2 ▲ Melt 2 oz (55 g) of the butter or margarine in a medium saucepan. Add the mushrooms and cook 5 minutes, stirring frequently. Stir in the flour and cook 3 minutes, stirring constantly. Pour in the milk, stock and white wine and bring to the boil, stirring. Reduce the heat and simmer 5 minutes.

3 Meanwhile, cook the spaghetti in a large pan of boiling salted water until just tender (see pack instructions for suggested cooking time). Drain.

4 ▼ Transfer the spaghetti to a mixing bowl. Pour in the mushroom sauce and mix well. Stir in the turkey, peas, half of the Parmesan and salt and pepper to taste. Transfer the mixture to the baking dish.

5 In a small bowl, combine the remaining Parmesan with the breadcrumbs. Sprinkle evenly over the turkey mixture. Dot with the remaining butter or margarine, cut into pieces. Bake until bubbling and golden, 30–40 minutes. Serve hot, in the baking dish.

Turkey Chilli (top), Turkey and Pasta Bake

Traditional Chicken Pie

SERVES 6

2 oz (55 g) butter or margarine

1 medium onion, chopped

3 carrots, cut into ½ in (1 cm) dice

1 parsnip, cut into ½ in (1 cm) dice

3 tbsp plain flour

12 fl oz (350 ml) chicken stock

3 fl oz (85 ml) medium sherry

3 fl oz (85 ml) dry white wine

6 fl oz (175 ml) whipping cream

3½ oz (100 g) frozen peas, thawed

12 oz (350 g) cooked chicken meat, in chunks

1 tsp dried thyme

1 tbsp finely chopped fresh parsley

salt and pepper

FOR THE PASTRY

5½ oz (165 g) plain flour

½ tsp salt

4 oz (115 g) lard or vegetable fat

2–3 tbsp iced water

1 egg

2 tbsp milk

1 ▲ For the pastry, sift the flour and salt into a mixing bowl. Using a pastry blender, cut in the fat until the mixture resembles coarse breadcrumbs. Sprinkle in the water, 1 tablespoon at a time, tossing lightly with a fork until the dough forms a ball. Dust with flour, wrap and refrigerate until required.

2 Preheat a 400°F/200°C/Gas 6 oven.

3 ▲ Heat half of the butter or margarine in a saucepan. Add the onion, carrots and parsnip and cook until softened, about 10 minutes. Remove the vegetables from the pan with a slotted spoon.

4 ▲ Melt the remaining butter or margarine in the saucepan. Add the flour and cook 5 minutes, stirring constantly. Stir in the stock, sherry and white wine. Bring the sauce to the boil, and continue boiling for 1 minute, stirring constantly.

5 ▲ Add the cream, peas, chicken, thyme and parsley to the sauce. Season to taste with salt and pepper. Simmer 1 minute, stirring.

6 ▼ Transfer the chicken mixture to a 3½ pt (2 litre) shallow baking dish.

7 On a lightly floured surface, roll out the pastry to ½ in (1 cm) thickness. Lay the pastry over the baking dish and trim off the excess. Dampen the rim of the dish. With a fork, press the pastry to the rim to seal.

8 Cut decorative shapes from the pastry trimmings.

9 ▲ Lightly whisk the egg with the milk. Brush the pastry all over with the egg wash. Arrange the pastry shapes in an attractive design on top. Brush again with the egg wash. Make 1 or 2 holes in the crust so steam can escape during baking.

10 Bake the pie until the pastry is golden brown, about 35 minutes. Serve hot.

Mexican Chicken

SERVES 4

1 × 3 lb (1.35 kg) chicken
1 tsp salt
12 taco shells
1 small head of iceberg lettuce, shredded
6 oz (170 g) tomatoes, chopped
8 fl oz (250 ml) soured cream
4 oz (115 g) Cheddar cheese, grated

FOR THE SAUCE

8 fl oz (250 ml) fresh tomatoes, skinned, cooked and sieved
1–2 garlic cloves, crushed
½ tsp cider vinegar
½ tsp dried oregano
½ tsp ground cumin
1–2 tbsp mild chilli powder

1 Put the chicken in a large pot and add the salt and enough water to cover. Bring to the boil. Reduce the heat and simmer until the chicken is thoroughly cooked, about 45 minutes. Remove the chicken and let cool. Reserve 4 fl oz (125 ml) of the chicken stock for the sauce.

2 ▲ Remove the chicken meat from the bones, discarding all skin. Chop the meat coarsely.

3 For the sauce, combine all the ingredients with the stock in a saucepan and bring to the boil. Stir in the chicken meat. Simmer until the sauce thickens considerably, about 20 minutes, stirring occasionally.

4 Preheat a 350°F/180°C/Gas 4 oven.

5 ▲ Spread out the taco shells on 2 baking trays. Heat in the oven for 7 minutes.

6 Meanwhile, put the shredded lettuce, chopped tomatoes, soured cream and grated cheese in individual serving dishes.

7 ▲ To serve, spoon a little of the chicken mixture into each taco shell. Garnish with the lettuce, tomatoes, soured cream and cheese.

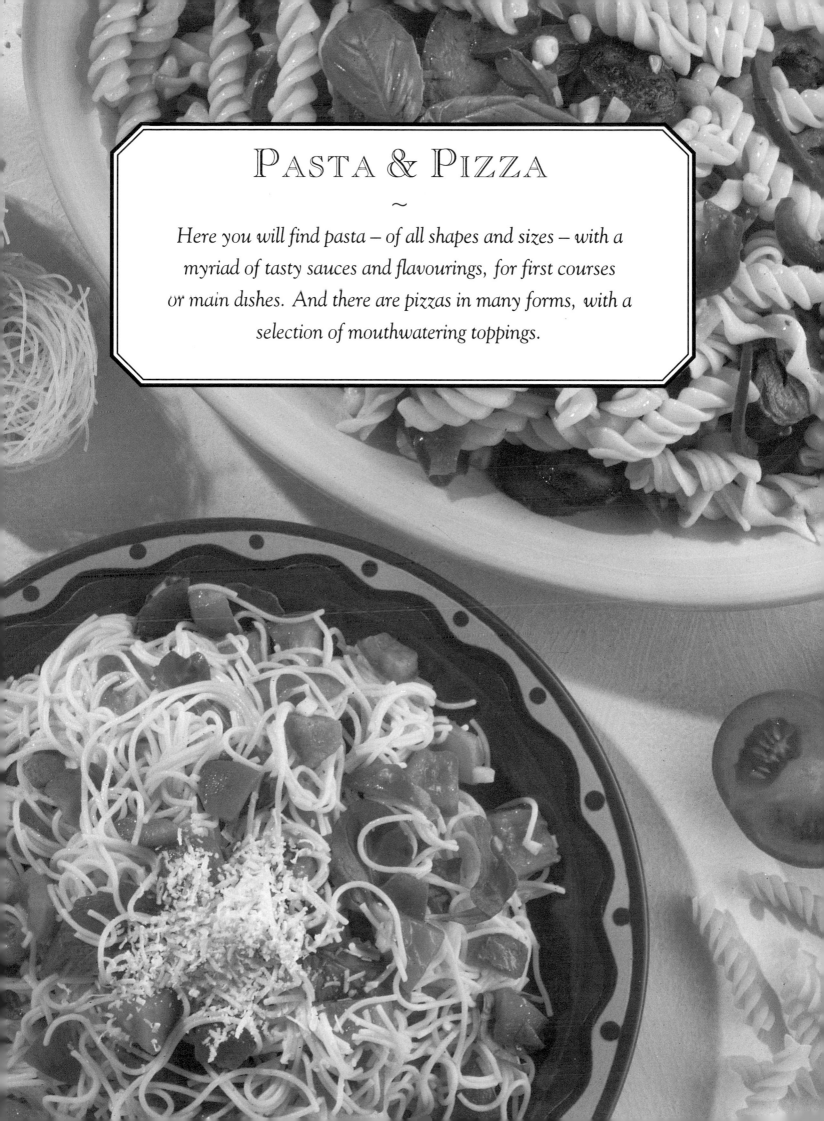

PASTA & PIZZA

~

Here you will find pasta – of all shapes and sizes – with a myriad of tasty sauces and flavourings, for first courses or main dishes. And there are pizzas in many forms, with a selection of mouthwatering toppings.

Spicy Cheese Lasagne

SERVES 8

8 oz (225 g) lasagne

2 oz (55 g) butter or margarine

1 large onion, finely chopped

3 garlic cloves, crushed

1½ tbsp chopped green chilli pepper

2 oz (55 g) plain flour

1¾ pt (1 litre) milk

1¼ pt (750 ml) canned chopped
 tomatoes

1 large courgette, sliced

½ tsp crushed dried chilli pepper

salt and pepper

12 oz (350 g) Cheddar cheese, grated

1 Preheat a 375°F/190°C/Gas 5 oven.
Grease a 13 × 9 in (33 × 23 cm) dish.

2 Put the lasagne sheets, one at a
time, in a bowl of hot water, and let
soak for 10–15 minutes.

3 ▲ Melt the butter or margarine in
a large saucepan. Add the onion,
garlic and chopped chilli and cook
until softened, about 5 minutes.

4 Stir in the flour and cook 3
minutes, stirring constantly. Pour in
the milk and bring to the boil,
stirring. Reduce the heat to low and
simmer gently until thickened, about
5 minutes, stirring occasionally.

5 Stir the tomatoes, courgettes, and
dried chilli pepper into the sauce.
Season with salt and pepper.

6 Spoon a little of the sauce into the
prepared baking dish and spread it out
evenly over the bottom. Cover with a
layer of lasagne.

7 ▲ Add one-third of the remaining
sauce and one-third of the cheese.
Repeat the layers until all the
ingredients are used.

8 Bake until the top is golden and
bubbling, about 45 minutes. Serve
hot, in the dish.

Spaghetti with Rich Tomato Sauce

SERVES 4

12 oz (350 g) spaghetti

4 garlic cloves, crushed

10–15 sun-dried tomatoes preserved in
 oil, drained and chopped

5 oz (140 g) black olives, stoned

4 fl oz (125 ml) extra-virgin olive oil

3 beef tomatoes, peeled, seeded and
 chopped

3 tbsp capers, drained

3 tbsp chopped fresh basil, plus leaves
 for garnishing, or 1 tsp dried basil

salt and pepper

1 Cook the spaghetti in a large pan of
boiling salted water until just tender
to the bite (check packet instructions
for timing). Drain well.

2 ▲ In a food processor or blender,
combine the garlic, sun-dried
tomatoes and half the olives. Process
until finely chopped.

3 With the motor running, slowly
add the olive oil. Continue processing
until thickened.

4 ▼ Transfer the mixture to a mixing
bowl. Stir in the fresh tomatoes,
capers and basil. Season with salt and
pepper to taste.

5 Return the spaghetti to the
saucepan and add the tomato sauce.
Toss well. Serve immediately,
garnished with the remaining olives
and fresh basil leaves, if wished.

Spicy Cheese Lasagne (top), Spaghetti with Rich Tomato Sauce

Pasta with Chicken and Sausage Sauce

SERVES 4

3 tbsp olive oil

1 lb (450 g) skinless boneless chicken breasts, cut into ½ in (1 cm) pieces

3 small spicy cooked sausages, cut diagonally into ½ in (1 cm) slices

salt and pepper

6 spring onions, cut diagonally into ¼ in (5 mm) lengths

10 sun-dried tomatoes preserved in oil, drained and chopped

8 fl oz (250 ml) canned chopped tomatoes

1 medium-sized courgette, cut diagonally into ¼ in (5 mm) slices

12 oz (350 g) bow-tie pasta (farfalle)

1 ▼ Heat the olive oil in a frying pan. Add the chicken and sausage pieces with a little salt and pepper and cook until browned, about 10 minutes. With a slotted spoon, remove the chicken and sausage from the pan and drain on kitchen paper.

2 ▲ Add the spring onions and sun-dried tomatoes to the pan and cook until softened, about 5 minutes.

3 ▲ Stir in the canned tomatoes and cook until thickened, about 5 minutes.

4 ▲ Add the courgette and return the chicken and sausage to the pan. Cook 5 minutes longer.

5 Cook the pasta in a large pan of boiling salted water until just tender (check packet instructions for timing). Drain well.

6 Serve the pasta with the chicken and sausage sauce.

Pasta with Spinach, Bacon and Mushrooms

SERVES 4

6 rashers of bacon, cut in small pieces
½ small onion, finely chopped
8 oz (225 g) small mushrooms, quartered
1 lb (450 g) fresh spinach leaves, stems removed
¼ tsp grated nutmeg
salt and pepper
12 oz (350 g) pasta shells
2 tbsp freshly grated Parmesan cheese

1 ▼ In a frying pan, cook the bacon until it is browned and the fat is rendered. Drain the bacon on kitchen paper, then put it in a bowl.

2 Add the onion to the bacon fat in the pan and cook until softened, about 5 minutes.

3 ▲ Add the mushrooms to the pan and cook until lightly browned, about 5 minutes, stirring frequently. With a slotted spoon, transfer the onion and mushrooms to the bacon in the bowl. Pour off the bacon fat from the frying pan.

4 ▼ Add the spinach to the pan and cook over a medium heat until wilted, stirring constantly.

5 Sprinkle with the nutmeg. Raise the heat to high and cook briskly, stirring to evaporate excess liquid from the spinach. Transfer the spinach to a board and chop it coarsely. Return it to the pan.

6 ▲ Return the bacon, mushrooms and onion to the pan and stir to mix with the spinach. Season with salt and pepper. Set aside.

7 Cook the pasta in a large pan of boiling salted water until just tender (check packet instructions for timing). Just before the pasta is ready, reheat the spinach mixture.

8 Drain the pasta well and return to the saucepan. Add the spinach mixture and toss well to mix. Sprinkle with Parmesan cheese before serving.

Pasta with Fresh Basil Sauce

SERVES 4

about 2 oz (55 g) chopped fresh basil

about 1 oz (30 g) chopped fresh parsley

1½ oz (45 g) Parmesan cheese, freshly grated

2 garlic cloves

2 oz (55 g) butter or margarine, at room temperature

2 fl oz (65 ml) extra-virgin olive oil

salt

12 oz (350 g) mixed green and white fettucine or tagliatelle

2 oz (55 g) pine kernels, toasted

fresh basil leaves, for garnishing

1 ▲ In a food processor or blender, combine the basil, parsley, Parmesan and garlic. Process until finely chopped.

2 Add the butter or margarine and process to mix well.

3 ▼ With the machine running, slowly add the olive oil. Season with salt to taste.

4 Cook the pasta in a large pan of boiling salted water until just tender (check packet instructions for timing). Drain well.

5 Toss the hot pasta with the basil sauce. Sprinkle with the pine kernels, garnish with basil and serve.

Pasta Quills with Cheesy Aubergine Sauce

SERVES 6

1¼ lb (575 g) aubergine, cut into ½ in (1 cm) cubes

salt and pepper

3 tbsp olive oil

½ oz (15 g) butter or margarine

1 garlic clove, chopped

16 fl oz (450 ml) canned chopped tomatoes

12 oz (350 g) pasta quills (penne)

4 oz (115 g) firm goat cheese, cubed

3 tbsp shredded fresh basil, or 1 tsp dried basil

1 Put the aubergine cubes in a large colander and sprinkle them lightly with salt. Let drain at least 30 minutes.

2 Rinse the aubergine under cold water and drain well. Dry on kitchen paper.

3 Heat the oil and butter or margarine in a large saucepan. Add the aubergine and fry until just golden on all sides, stirring frequently.

4 ▲ Stir in the garlic and tomatoes. Simmer until thickened, about 15 minutes. Season with salt and pepper.

5 ▲ Cook the pasta quills in a large pan of boiling salted water until just tender (check packet instructions for timing). Drain well and transfer to a warmed serving bowl.

6 Add the aubergine sauce, goat cheese and basil to the pasta and toss well together. Serve immediately.

Pasta with Fresh Basil Sauce (top), Pasta Quills with Cheesy Aubergine Sauce

Pasta Spirals with Spicy Sausage

SERVES 4

3 tbsp olive oil

1 lb (450 g) chorizo or other spicy cooked sausages, cut diagonally in ½ in (1 cm) slices

1 onion, chopped

1 garlic clove, crushed

2 red peppers, seeded and sliced

12 oz (350 g) drained canned sweetcorn, or frozen sweetcorn, thawed

salt and pepper

12 oz (350 g) pasta spirals (fusilli)

1 tbsp chopped fresh basil, or ½ tsp dried basil

fresh basil leaves, for garnishing

1 Heat 1 tablespoon of the oil in a frying pan. Add the sausage slices and brown them on both sides.

2 Remove the sausage from the pan with a slotted spoon and drain on kitchen paper.

3 ▲ Heat the remaining oil in the pan and add the onion, garlic and peppers. Cook until softened, about 5 minutes, stirring frequently.

4 ▲ Stir the sausage and sweetcorn into the pepper mixture and heat through, about 5 minutes. Season with salt and pepper.

5 Cook the pasta in boiling salted water until just tender (check packet instructions for timing). Drain well and return to the pan.

6 Add the sausage sauce and basil to the pasta. Toss together well, garnish with basil and serve immediately.

Pasta with Tomato and Lime Sauce

SERVES 4

1 lb (450 g) very ripe tomatoes, peeled and chopped

1 small bunch of tender, young rocket or spinach leaves

4 garlic cloves, crushed

grated rind of ½ lime

juice of 2 limes

¼ tsp chilli sauce

12 oz (350 g) thin spaghetti (capellini)

2 fl oz (65 ml) olive oil

salt and pepper

freshly grated Parmesan cheese, for serving

1 ▼ Combine the tomatoes, rocket, garlic, lime rind and juice and chilli sauce. Stir well to mix. Set aside for 20–30 minutes.

2 Cook the pasta in boiling salted water until just tender (check packet instructions for timing). Drain and return to the pan.

3 ▲ Add the olive oil and tomato and lime sauce to the pasta. Toss well together. Season with salt and pepper. Add Parmesan cheese to taste, toss again and serve.

Pasta Spirals with Spicy Sausage (top), Pasta with Tomato and Lime Sauce

Macaroni Cheese

SERVES 4

4 oz (115 g) macaroni

2 oz (55 g) butter or margarine

1 oz (30 g) plain flour

1 pt (575 ml) milk

6 oz (170 g) Cheddar cheese, grated

3 tbsp finely chopped fresh parsley

salt and pepper

3½ oz (100 g) dry breadcrumbs

1½ oz (45 g) Parmesan cheese, freshly grated

1 Preheat a 350°F/180°C/Gas 4 oven. Grease a 10 in (25 cm) gratin dish.

2 Cook the macaroni in boiling salted water until just tender (check packet instructions for timing). Drain well.

3 Melt the butter or margarine in a saucepan. Add the flour and cook 2 minutes, stirring. Stir in the milk. Bring to a boil, stirring constantly, and simmer until thickened, about 5 minutes.

4 ▲ Remove the pan from the heat. Add the macaroni, Cheddar cheese and parsley to the sauce and mix well. Season with salt and pepper.

5 Transfer the mixture to the prepared gratin dish, spreading it out evenly with a spoon.

6 ▲ Toss together the breadcrumbs and Parmesan cheese with a fork. Sprinkle over the macaroni.

7 Bake until the top is golden brown and the macaroni mixture is bubbling, 30–35 minutes.

Noodle and Vegetable Bake

SERVES 10

1 lb (450 g) egg noodles

3 oz (85 g) butter or margarine

1 onion, chopped

3 garlic cloves, chopped

3 carrots, grated

12 oz (350 g) small mushrooms, quartered

3 eggs, beaten

12 oz (350 g) cottage cheese

8 fl oz (250 ml) soured cream

2 courgettes, finely chopped in a food processor

3 tbsp chopped fresh basil, or 1 tbsp dried basil

salt and pepper

fresh basil leaves, for garnishing

1 Preheat a 350°F/180°C/Gas 4 oven. Grease a 13 × 9 in (33 × 23 cm) baking dish.

2 Cook the pasta in boiling salted water until just tender (check packet instructions for timing). Drain and rinse with cold water. Transfer to a mixing bowl.

3 Melt two-thirds of the butter or margarine in a frying pan. Add the onion, garlic and carrots and cook until tender, about 10 minutes, stirring frequently.

4 ▲ Stir in the mushrooms and cook 5 minutes longer. Add the vegetables to the noodles in the mixing bowl.

5 In a small bowl, combine the eggs, cottage cheese, soured cream, courgettes, basil and salt and pepper to taste. Mix well.

6 ▲ Add the cottage cheese mixture to the noodles and mix well. Transfer to the prepared baking dish. Dot the top with the remaining butter or margarine.

7 Cover the dish with foil. Bake until the casserole is set, about 1 hour. Serve hot, in the baking dish, garnished with basil leaves.

Macaroni Cheese (top), Noodle and Vegetable Bake

Pitta-Bread Pizzas

SERVES 4

4 × 6 in (15 cm) round pitta breads,
 split in half horizontally

2 fl oz (65 ml) olive oil

salt and pepper

1 small red pepper, seeded and sliced

1 small yellow pepper, seeded and sliced

8 oz (225 g) small red potatoes, cooked
 and sliced

1 tbsp chopped fresh rosemary, or 1 tsp
 dried rosemary

1½ oz (45 g) Parmesan cheese, freshly
 grated

1 Preheat a 350°F/180°C/Gas 4 oven.

2 ▼ Place the pitta rounds on a baking tray. Brush them on both sides with 2 tablespoons of the oil. Sprinkle with salt. Bake until pale golden and crisp, about 10 minutes.

3 ▲ Heat the remaining oil in a frying pan. Add the peppers and cook until softened, about 5 minutes, stirring frequently.

4 ▲ Add the potatoes and rosemary to the peppers. Heat through, about 3 minutes, stirring well. Season with salt and pepper.

5 Preheat the grill.

6 ▲ Divide the pepper-potato mixture between the pitta rounds. Sprinkle with the Parmesan cheese and transfer to the grill pan.

7 Grill about 3 in (8 cm) from the heat until golden, 3–4 minutes.

Onion, Olive and Anchovy Pizza

SERVES 4

6 tbsp olive oil
1 lb (450 g) onions, thinly sliced
3 garlic cloves, crushed
1 bay leaf
2 tsp dried thyme
salt and pepper
2 cans anchovy fillets, drained and blotted dry on kitchen paper
12 olives, mixed black and green
FOR THE PIZZA DOUGH
4 oz (115 g) wholewheat flour
3 oz (85 g) plain flour
1¼ tsp active dry yeast
⅛ tsp sugar
5 fl oz (150 ml) tepid water
2 tbsp olive oil
½ tsp salt

1 For the pizza dough, in a food processor combine the flours, yeast and sugar. With the motor running, pour in the tepid water. Turn the motor off. Add the oil and salt. Process until a ball of dough is formed.

2 Put the dough in an oiled bowl and turn it to coat with oil. Cover and let rise until doubled in size.

3 ▲ Heat 3 tablespoons of the oil in a frying pan. Add the onions, garlic and herbs. Cook over a low heat until the onions are very soft and the moisture has evaporated, about 45 minutes. Season with salt and pepper.

4 Preheat the oven to the highest setting. Oil a 13 × 9 in (33 × 23 cm) baking tray.

5 ▼ Transfer the risen dough onto a lightly floured surface. Punch down the dough and knead it briefly. Roll it out into a rectangle to fit the baking tray. Lay the dough on the tray and press it up the edges of the tray.

6 Brush the dough with 1 tablespoon olive oil. Discard the bay leaf, and spoon the onion mixture onto the dough. Spread it out evenly, leaving a ½ in (1 cm) border around the edge.

7 ▲ Arrange the anchovies and olives on top of the onions. Drizzle the remaining 2 tablespoons olive oil over the top.

8 Bake the pizza until the edges are puffed and browned, 15–20 minutes.

Broccoli and Goat Cheese Pizza

SERVES 2–3

8 oz (225 g) broccoli florets
2 tbsp cornmeal, or polenta
4 fl oz (125 ml) fresh tomatoes, skinned, cooked and sieved
6 cherry tomatoes, halved
12 black olives, stoned
4 oz (115 g) goat cheese, cut into pieces
1½ oz (45 g) Parmesan cheese, grated
1 tbsp olive oil
FOR THE PIZZA DOUGH
8–9 oz (225–250 g) plain flour
1 package active dry yeast (¼ oz/7.5 g)
⅛ tsp sugar
5 fl oz (150 ml) tepid water
2 tbsp olive oil
½ tsp salt

1 For the pizza dough, combine 3 oz (85 g) of the flour, the yeast and sugar in a food processor. With the motor running, pour in the water. Turn the motor off. Add the oil, 5 oz (140 g) of the remaining flour and the salt.

2 ▲ Process until a ball of dough is formed, adding more water, 1 teaspoon at a time, if the dough is too dry, or the remaining flour, 1 tablespoon at a time, if it is too wet.

3 ▲ Put the dough in an oiled bowl and turn it so the ball of dough is oiled all over. Cover the bowl and let the dough rise in a warm place until doubled in size, about 1 hour.

4 ▲ Meanwhile, cook the broccoli florets in boiling salted water or steam them until just tender, about 5 minutes. Drain well and set aside.

5 Preheat the oven to the highest setting. Oil a 12 in (30 cm) round pizza pan and sprinkle with the cornmeal.

6 When the dough has risen, turn out onto a lightly floured surface. Punch down the dough to deflate it, and knead it briefly.

~ **COOK'S TIP** ~

If more convenient, the pizza dough can be used as soon as it is made, without any rising.

7 ▲ Roll out the dough to a 12 in (30 cm) round. Lay the dough on the pizza pan and press it down evenly.

8 ▲ Spread the tomato sauce evenly onto the pizza base, leaving a rim of dough uncovered around the edge about ½ in (1 cm) wide.

9 ▲ Arrange the broccoli florets, tomatoes, and olives on the tomato sauce and sprinkle with the cheeses. Drizzle the olive oil over the top.

10 Bake until the cheese melts and the edge of the pizza base is puffed and browned, 10–15 minutes.

Pizza Toasts with Cheesy Topping

SERVES 4

2 small aubergines, cut across into thin slices (about 8 oz/225 g)

1 tbsp salt

4 fl oz (125 ml) olive oil

1 garlic clove, crushed with the side of a knife

8 slices French bread, ½ in (1 cm) thick

8 oz (225 g) Mozzarella cheese, cut into 8 slices

3 tbsp chopped fresh chives

3 tbsp chopped fresh basil

1 ▲ Put the aubergine slices in a colander and sprinkle with the salt. Let stand at least 30 minutes to drain. Rinse the aubergine slices under cold water, then blot dry with kitchen paper.

2 Heat half the olive oil in a frying pan. Add the aubergine slices and fry until golden brown, about 5 minutes on each side. Add more oil if necessary when the slices are turned over. Drain on kitchen paper.

3 Preheat a 325°F/170°C/Gas 3 oven.

4 ▲ In a small bowl, combine the remaining olive oil and the garlic. Brush both sides of the bread slices with the garlic oil. Place the slices on a baking tray. Bake until golden brown, about 10 minutes.

5 Preheat the grill.

6 ▲ Top each slice of garlic bread with a slice of aubergine and a slice of Mozzarella. Arrange on a baking tray.

7 Grill about 3 in (8 cm) from the heat until the cheese melts, 5–7 minutes. Sprinkle the toasts with the chopped herbs before serving.

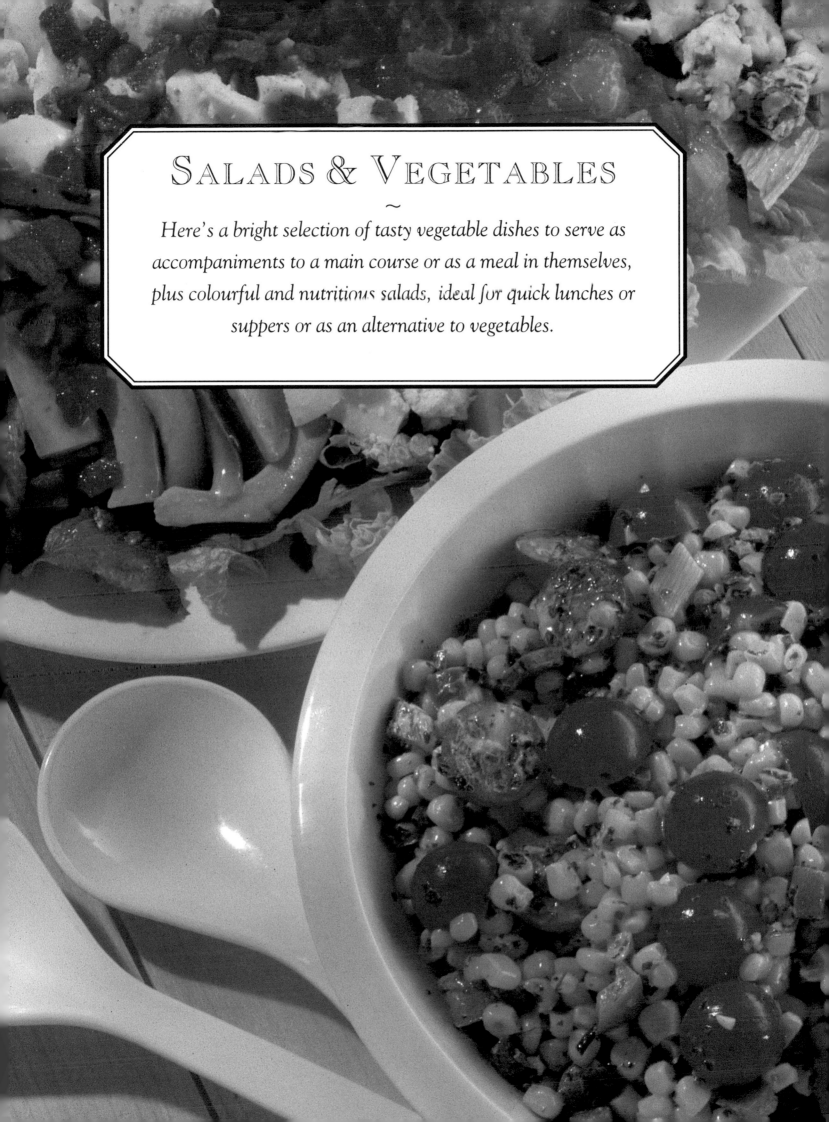

SALADS & VEGETABLES

~

Here's a bright selection of tasty vegetable dishes to serve as accompaniments to a main course or as a meal in themselves, plus colourful and nutritious salads, ideal for quick lunches or suppers or as an alternative to vegetables.

Caesar Salad

SERVES 4

2 eggs

1 garlic clove, crushed

½ tsp salt

4 fl oz (125 ml) olive oil

juice of 1 lemon

¼ tsp Worcestershire sauce

1 lb (450 g) cos lettuce, torn into bite-sized pieces

1½ oz (45 g) Parmesan cheese, freshly grated

pepper

8 canned anchovy fillets, drained and blotted dry on kitchen paper (optional)

FOR THE CROUTONS

1 garlic clove

¼ tsp salt

2 fl oz (65 ml) olive oil

4–6 slices French bread, cubed

1 Preheat a 350°F/180°C/Gas 4 oven.

2 ▲ For the croûtons, crush the garlic with the salt in a mixing bowl and mix in the oil. Add the bread cubes to the bowl and toss to coat with the garlic oil.

3 Spread the bread cubes on a baking tray. Bake until golden brown, 20–25 minutes.

4 Meanwhile, put the eggs in a small pan of boiling water and simmer gently for 7 minutes. Transfer the eggs to a bowl of cold water and shell them as soon as they are cool enough to handle.

5 ▼ Mash the garlic clove with the salt in the bottom of a salad bowl. Whisk in the olive oil, lemon juice and Worcestershire sauce.

6 Add the lettuce to the salad bowl and toss well to coat with the dressing.

7 Add the Parmesan cheese and season with pepper. Add the croûtons and toss well to combine.

8 Cut the hard-boiled eggs in quarters. Arrange on top of the salad with the anchovies, if using. Serve immediately.

Green Salad with Blue Cheese Dressing

SERVES 6

4 handfuls mixed salad leaves, torn in bite-size pieces

1 small bunch of lamb's lettuce (mâche), rocket or watercress

FOR THE DRESSING

4 fl oz (125 ml) plain yoghurt

1½ tsp white wine vinegar

½ tsp sugar

1 tbsp fresh lemon juice

1 garlic clove, crushed

1 oz (30 g) blue cheese, crumbled

1 ▼ For the dressing, combine the yoghurt, wine vinegar, sugar, lemon juice and garlic in a small bowl and mix well. Fold in the cheese. The dressing should be lumpy.

2 ▲ Put the salad leaves in a salad bowl. Add the dressing and toss until all the leaves are coated. Serve immediately.

Caesar Salad (top), Green Salad with Blue Cheese Dressing

Egg, Bacon and Avocado Salad

SERVES 4

1 large head of cos lettuce, sliced into strips across the leaves

8 rashers of bacon, fried until crisp and crumbled

2 large avocados, peeled and diced

6 hard-boiled eggs, chopped

2 beef tomatoes, peeled, seeded and chopped

6 oz (170 g) blue cheese, crumbled

FOR THE DRESSING

1 garlic clove, crushed

1 tsp sugar

½ tbsp fresh lemon juice

1½ tbsp red wine vinegar

4 fl oz (125 ml) groundnut oil

salt and pepper

1 For the dressing, combine all the ingredients in a screwtop jar and shake well.

2 ▲ On a large rectangular or oval platter, spread out the lettuce to make a bed.

3 ▲ Reserve the bacon, and arrange the remaining ingredients in rows, beginning with the avocados. Sprinkle the bacon on top.

4 Pour the dressing over the salad just before serving.

Spicy Sweetcorn Salad

SERVES 4

2 tbsp vegetable oil

1 lb (450 g) drained canned sweetcorn, or frozen sweetcorn, thawed

1 green pepper, seeded and diced

1 small fresh red chilli pepper, seeded and finely diced

4 spring onions, cut diagonally into ½ in (1 cm) lengths

3 tbsp chopped fresh parsley

8 oz (225 g) cherry tomatoes, halved

salt and pepper

FOR THE DRESSING

½ tsp sugar

2 tbsp white wine vinegar

½ tsp Dijon mustard

1 tbsp chopped fresh basil, or 1 tsp dried basil

1 tbsp mayonnaise

¼ tsp chilli sauce

1 Heat the oil in a frying pan. Add the sweetcorn, pepper, chilli pepper and spring onions. Cook over a medium heat until softened, about 5 minutes, stirring frequently.

2 ▲ Transfer the vegetables to a salad bowl. Stir in the parsley and tomatoes.

3 ▲ For the dressing, combine all the ingredients in a small bowl and whisk together. Pour the dressing over the sweetcorn mixture. Season with salt and pepper. Toss well to combine, and serve.

Egg, Bacon and Avocado Salad (top), Spicy Sweetcorn Salad

Spinach and Bacon Salad

SERVES 4

1 hard-boiled egg

3 fl oz (85 ml) white wine vinegar

1 tsp Dijon mustard

2 tbsp vegetable or olive oil

salt and pepper

1 lb (450 g) fresh young spinach leaves

2 oz (55 g) small mushrooms, sliced

3 rashers of bacon

1 medium onion, chopped

2 garlic cloves, crushed

1 Separate the egg yolk and white. Chop the egg white and set aside.

2 ▲ To make the dressing, press the egg yolk through a sieve into a bowl. Whisk in the vinegar, mustard, oil and salt and pepper to taste.

3 Put the spinach in a salad bowl with the mushrooms.

4 In a small frying pan, fry the bacon until crisp. Remove the bacon and drain on kitchen paper.

5 ▼ When cool, crumble the bacon over the spinach.

6 Add the onion and garlic to the bacon fat in the frying pan and cook until softened, about 5 minutes, stirring frequently.

7 Pour the onion and garlic over the spinach, with the bacon fat. Add the dressing and toss well to combine. Sprinkle the egg white on top and serve immediately.

Warm Red Cabbage Salad with Spicy Sausage

SERVES 4

1 lb (450 g) red cabbage, cut in wedges and cored

2 fl oz (65 ml) olive oil

2 shallots or 1 small onion, chopped

2 garlic cloves, chopped

3 tbsp cider vinegar

4 oz (115 g) chorizo or other cooked spicy sausage, cut diagonally in ¼ in (5 mm) slices

salt and pepper

2 tbsp chopped fresh chives

2 tbsp chopped fresh parsley

1 Slice the cabbage wedges very thinly across the leaves.

2 ▲ Heat the oil in a frying pan. Add the shallots and garlic and cook until softened, about 4 minutes. Transfer from the pan to a salad bowl using a slotted spoon.

3 Add the cabbage to the hot oil and cook until wilted, about 10 minutes, stirring occasionally. Add 1 tablespoon of the vinegar and cook 1 minute longer, stirring. Transfer the cabbage and the oil from the pan to the salad bowl.

4 ▼ Add the sausage slices to the pan and fry until well browned. Transfer the sausage to the salad bowl using the slotted spoon.

5 Pour the remaining vinegar over the salad and toss well to combine. Season with salt and pepper. Sprinkle with the chopped herbs and serve.

Spinach and Bacon Salad (top), Warm Red Cabbage Salad with Spicy Sausage

Mashed Potatoes with Garlic

SERVES 6

2–3 heads of garlic, according to taste, cloves separated

2 oz (55 g) butter or margarine

2½ lb (1.2 kg) potatoes, peeled and quartered

salt and pepper

4 fl oz (125 ml) whipping cream

3 tbsp chopped fresh chives

1 Drop the garlic cloves into a pan of boiling water and boil 2 minutes. Drain and peel.

2 ▲ Melt half the butter or margarine in a small saucepan over a low heat. Add the peeled garlic. Cover and cook until very soft, 20–25 minutes, stirring frequently.

3 Meanwhile, cook the potatoes in boiling salted water until tender, 15–20 minutes. Drain well and return to the pan. Set over medium heat to evaporate excess moisture, 2–3 minutes.

4 ▲ Push the potatoes through a potato ricer or mash them with a potato masher. Return them to the saucepan and beat in the remaining butter or margarine, in two batches. Season with salt and pepper.

5 ▲ Remove the pan of garlic from the heat and mash the garlic and butter together with a fork until smooth. Stir in the cream. Return to the heat and bring just to the boil.

6 Beat the garlic cream into the potatoes, 1 tablespoon at a time. Reheat the potatoes if necessary.

7 Fold most of the chives into the potatoes. Transfer the potatoes to a warmed serving bowl and sprinkle the remaining chives on top.

Candied Sweet Potatoes

SERVES 8

3 lb (1.35 kg) sweet potatoes, peeled

1½ oz (45 g) butter or margarine

4 fl oz (125 ml) maple syrup

¾ tsp ground ginger

1 tbsp fresh lemon juice

1 Preheat a 375°F/190°C/Gas 5 oven. Grease a large shallow baking dish.

2 ▲ Cut the potatoes in ½ in (1 cm) slices. Cook them in boiling water for 10 minutes. Drain. Let cool.

3 ▲ Melt the butter or margarine in a small saucepan over a medium heat. Stir in the maple syrup until well combined. Stir in the ginger. Simmer 1 minute, then add the lemon juice.

4 ▼ Arrange the potato slices in one layer in the prepared baking dish, overlapping them slightly.

5 ▲ Drizzle the maple syrup mixture evenly over the potatoes. Bake until the potatoes are tender and glazed, 30–35 minutes, spooning the cooking liquid over them once or twice.

Brussels Sprouts with Chestnuts

Serves 6

1 lb (450 g) Brussels sprouts, trimmed

4 oz (115 g) butter or margarine

3 celery sticks, cut diagonally in ½ in (1 cm) lengths

1 large onion, thinly sliced

1 × 14 oz (400 g) can whole chestnuts in brine, drained and rinsed

¼ tsp grated nutmeg

salt and pepper

grated rind of 1 lemon

2 ▲ Melt the butter or margarine in a frying pan over low heat. Add the celery and onion and cook until softened, about 5 minutes.

1 ▲ Drop the Brussels sprouts into a pan of boiling salted water and cook 3–4 minutes. Drain well.

3 ▲ Raise the heat to medium and add the chestnuts and Brussels sprouts to the frying pan.

4 Stir in the nutmeg and salt and pepper to taste. Cook until piping hot, about 2 minutes, stirring frequently.

5 ▲ Stir in the grated lemon rind. Transfer to a warmed serving dish.

~ **VARIATION** ~

For a tasty alternative, substitute grated orange rind for the lemon rind, especially when serving with pork or turkey.

Green Peas and Baby Onions

Serves 6

½ oz (15 g) butter or margarine

12 baby onions, peeled

1 small butterhead lettuce, shredded

10 oz (300 g) shelled fresh green peas or frozen peas, thawed

1 tsp sugar

2 tbsp water

salt and pepper

2 sprigs fresh mint

1 Melt the butter or margarine in a frying pan. Add the onions and cook over medium heat until they just begin to colour, about 10 minutes.

2 ▼ Add the lettuce, peas, sugar and water. Season with salt and pepper. Bring to a boil. Reduce the heat to low, cover and simmer until the peas are tender, about 15 minutes for fresh peas and 10 minutes for frozen peas, stirring occasionally.

3 ▲ Strip the mint leaves from the stems. Chop finely with a sharp knife. Stir the mint into the peas. Transfer to a warmed serving dish.

Brussels Sprouts with Chestnuts (top), Green Peas and Baby Onions

Creamy Sweetcorn with Peppers

Serves 4

1 oz (30 g) butter or margarine

1 small red pepper, seeded and finely diced

1 small green pepper, seeded and finely diced

4 corn cobs, trimmed

4 fl oz (125 ml) whipping cream

salt and pepper

1 ▲ Melt the butter or margarine in a saucepan. Add the peppers and cook 5 minutes, stirring occasionally.

2 ▼ Cut the kernels off the corn cobs. Scrape the cobs with the back of a knife to extract the milky liquid. Alternatively, use a corn scraper to remove the kernels and liquid.

~ **VARIATION** ~

1 lb (450 g) frozen sweetcorn, thawed, can be substituted if fresh corn cobs are not available.

3 ▲ Add the sweetcorn with the liquid to the saucepan. Stir in the cream. Bring to the boil and simmer until thickened and the sweetcorn is tender, 3–4 minutes. Season with salt and pepper.

Fried Okra

Serves 6

1½ lb (700 g) okra

2 oz (55 g) cornmeal, or polenta

⅛ tsp black pepper

3 fl oz (85 ml) bacon dripping or oil

¾ tsp salt

~ **COOK'S TIP** ~

When removing the stems of the okra, slice through the point where it joins the vegetable. Cutting into the vegetable allows the release of the viscous insides.

1 Wash the okra well and drain in a colander. Cut off the stems.

2 ▲ Combine the cornmeal and pepper in a mixing bowl. Add the still damp okra and toss to coat evenly with cornmeal.

3 ▼ Heat the bacon drippings or oil in a frying pan. Add the okra and fry until tender and golden, 4–5 minutes. Drain on kitchen paper.

4 Sprinkle the fried okra with the salt just before serving.

Creamy Sweetcorn with Peppers (top), Fried Okra

Mixed Rice Ring

SERVES 8

2 tbsp vegetable oil

1 large onion, chopped

12 oz (350 g) mixed long-grain and wild rice

2 pt (1.25 litres) chicken stock

2½ oz (75 g) currants

salt

6 spring onions, cut diagonally into ¼ in (5 mm) lengths

parsley sprigs, for garnishing

1 Oil a 2¾ pt (1.75 litre) ring.

2 ▼ Heat the oil in a large saucepan. Add the onion and cook until softened, about 5 minutes.

3 ▲ Add the rice to the pan and stir well to coat the rice with the oil.

4 ▲ Stir in the chicken stock and bring to the boil.

5 Reduce the heat to low. Stir the currants into the rice mixture. Add salt to taste. Cover and simmer until the rice is tender and the stock has been absorbed, about 20 minutes.

6 Drain the rice if necessary and transfer it to a mixing bowl. Stir in the spring onions.

7 ▲ Pack the rice mixture into the prepared mould. Unmould it onto a warmed serving platter. If you like, put parsley sprigs into the centre of the ring before serving.

Green and Orange Risotto

SERVES 4

2 pt (1.25 litres) chicken stock
1½ oz (45 g) butter or margarine
1 small onion, chopped
2 oz (55 g) peeled and coarsely grated acorn squash or pumpkin
9 oz (250 g) short-grain rice
1 courgette, quartered lengthwise and chopped
5 oz (140 g) frozen peas, thawed
1½ oz (45 g) Parmesan cheese, grated
salt and pepper

1 In a saucepan, bring the stock to a simmer. Keep it simmering gently.

2 Melt one-third of the butter or margarine in a heavy saucepan. Add the onion and cook until softened, about 5 minutes.

3 ▲ Add the grated squash to the onion. Cook 1 minute, stirring.

4 ▲ Add the rice and stir to coat all the grains well with butter. Cook 1 minute, stirring.

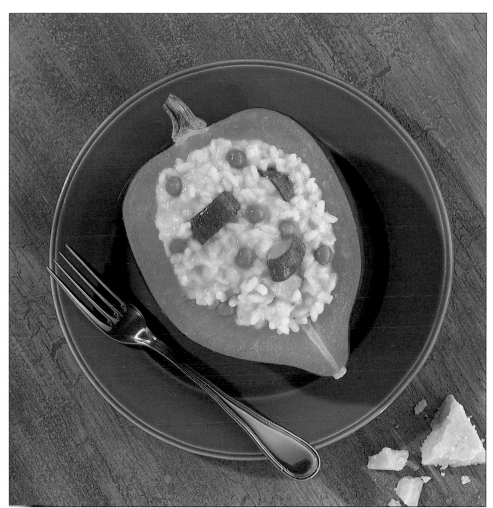

5 Add a ladleful of the simmering stock to the rice. Cook, stirring frequently, until the stock is absorbed. Continue adding the stock, one ladleful at a time, allowing each addition to be absorbed before adding the next, and stirring frequently.

6 ▲ After about 5 minutes, stir in the courgette pieces. After about 10 minutes, stir in the peas. The risotto will be cooked in about 20 minutes.

7 ▲ Remove the pan from the heat. Add the remaining butter or margarine and the Parmesan and stir well. Season with salt and pepper. If you like, serve in hollowed-out cooked acorn squash halves.

Couscous with Vegetables

SERVES 4

2 tbsp olive oil

8 button onions, peeled

1 red pepper, seeded and quartered

1 leek, cut across into 1 in (2.5 cm) lengths

¼ tsp saffron strands

½ tsp turmeric

¼ tsp cayenne pepper

1 tsp ground ginger

1 × 3 in (8 cm) cinnamon stick

3 large carrots, cut diagonally into 1 in (2.5 cm) lengths

1 swede, peeled and cubed

2 potatoes, peeled and quartered

1 × 16 oz (450 g) can chopped tomatoes

1¼ pt (750 ml) chicken stock

salt and pepper

2 courgettes, cut across into 1 in (2.5 cm) lengths

4 oz (115 g) whole green beans, trimmed

1 × 15 oz (420 g) can chick peas, drained

2 tbsp chopped fresh coriander

2 tbsp chopped fresh parsley

FOR THE COUSCOUS

1 pt (575 ml) water

½ tsp salt

9 oz (250 g) instant couscous

1 Heat the oil in a large saucepan or cast iron casserole. Add the onions, red pepper and leek. Cook for 2–3 minutes.

~ COOK'S TIP ~

This couscous makes a filling vegetarian meal, and the recipe can be doubled or tripled. When multiplying a recipe, increase spices by less and taste.

2 ▲ Stir in the saffron, turmeric, cayenne, ginger and cinnamon stick.

3 ▲ Add the carrots, swede, potatoes, tomatoes and chicken stock. Season with salt. Bring to the boil. Reduce the heat to low, cover and simmer until the vegetables are nearly tender, about 25 minutes.

4 ▲ Meanwhile, for the couscous, put the water and salt in a saucepan and bring to the boil. Stir in the couscous. Remove the pan from the heat, cover and set aside until all the liquid is absorbed, about 10 minutes.

5 ▲ Stir the courgettes, green beans and chick peas into the vegetable mixture. Simmer 5 minutes longer.

6 ▲ Stir in the herbs and add pepper to taste.

7 ▲ Lightly fluff the couscous grains with a fork. Pile the couscous in a mound in the middle of a shallow, round platter. Spoon the vegetables over the couscous and serve.

Red Beans and Rice

SERVES 4

1 onion, chopped
1 green pepper, seeded and chopped
4 rashers of bacon, chopped
1 garlic clove, chopped
6 oz (170 g) long-grain rice
2–3 tsp chilli powder
2 tsp fresh thyme leaves or ½ tsp dried thyme
16 fl oz (450 ml) canned chopped tomatoes
8 fl oz (250 ml) chicken or beef stock
salt and pepper
1 × 15 oz (420 g) can red kidney beans, drained and rinsed

1 ▼ In a medium saucepan, cook the onion, green pepper, bacon and garlic until the vegetables are softened and the bacon has rendered its fat, about 5 minutes.

2 ▲ Add the rice and stir until all the grains are coated with bacon fat. Stir in the chilli powder and cook 1 minute.

3 ▲ Add the thyme, chopped tomatoes and stock and stir well. Season with salt and pepper. Bring to the boil.

4 Reduce the heat to low, cover the pan and simmer until the rice is nearly tender, about 15 minutes.

5 ▲ Stir in the kidney beans. Cover again and simmer until the rice is tender and all the stock has been absorbed, about 5 minutes longer.

6 Fluff the rice and beans with a fork, then transfer to a warmed serving dish.

Nut Pilaf

SERVES 4

1 oz (30 g) butter or margarine
1 onion, finely chopped
12 oz (350 g) long-grain brown rice
½ tsp finely grated lemon rind
16 fl oz (450 ml) chicken stock
16 fl oz (450 ml) water
¼ tsp salt
4 spring onions, finely chopped
2 tbsp fresh lemon juice
1½ oz (45 g) pecan halves, toasted

1 ▲ Melt the butter or margarine in a medium saucepan. Add the onion and cook until softened, about 5 minutes.

2 ▲ Stir in the rice and cook 1 minute, stirring.

3 ▲ Add the lemon rind, chicken stock, water and salt and stir well. Bring to the boil. Reduce the heat to low, cover the pan and simmer until the rice is tender and all the liquid is absorbed, 30–35 minutes.

4 ▼ Remove the pan from the heat and let stand 5 minutes, still covered. Stir in the spring onions, lemon juice and pecan halves. Transfer to a warmed serving dish.

Spinach Moulds with Tomato Dressing

SERVES 6

1½ lb (700 g) frozen chopped spinach, thawed

1 oz (30 g) butter or margarine

3 oz (85 g) fresh breadcrumbs

salt and pepper

2 eggs

1 egg yolk

12 fl oz (350 ml) milk

3 tbsp freshly grated Parmesan cheese

fresh thyme sprigs, for garnishing

FOR THE DRESSING

5 tsp fresh lemon juice

1 tsp sugar

½ tsp whole-grain mustard

½ tsp fresh thyme leaves, or ⅛ tsp dried thyme

4 fl oz (125 ml) olive oil

3 tomatoes, peeled, seeded and diced

1 Preheat a 350°F/180°C/Gas 4 oven. Butter 6 ramekins. Place them in a shallow baking tin.

2 ▲ A handful at a time, squeeze the thawed spinach to remove as much water as possible.

3 Melt the butter or margarine in a saucepan. Stir in the spinach and cook 1 minute over a high heat, stirring.

4 ▲ Remove the pan from the heat. Stir the breadcrumbs into the spinach. Season with salt and pepper.

5 In a small bowl, beat the whole eggs with the egg yolk. Scald the milk in a small saucepan. Lightly beat it into the eggs.

6 ▲ Add the Parmesan cheese to the milk mixture and stir into the spinach mixture.

7 ▲ Spoon the mixture into the ramekins, dividing it evenly. Cover each ramekin tightly with foil.

8 ▲ Add hot water to the baking tin to come halfway up the sides of the ramekins. Bake until a knife inserted in a flan comes out clean, about 35 minutes.

9 ▲ Meanwhile, for the dressing, combine the lemon juice, sugar, mustard and thyme in a bowl. Whisk in the olive oil. Stir in the tomatoes and salt and pepper to taste.

10 To serve, unmould the flans onto individual plates. Spoon a little dressing over each flan and garnish with a sprig of fresh thyme.

~ COOK'S TIP ~

Fresh breadcrumbs are easy to make using a food processor. Remove and discard the crusts from several slices of bread. Tear the bread into smaller pieces and process.

Pasta-Stuffed Peppers

SERVES 4

6 rashers of bacon, chopped
1 small onion, chopped
12 fl oz (350 ml) canned chopped tomatoes
⅛ tsp crushed dried chilli peppers
2 oz (55 g) macaroni
6 oz (170 g) Mozzarella cheese, diced
12 black olives, stoned and thinly sliced
salt and pepper
2 large red peppers
2 large yellow peppers
2 tbsp olive oil

1 Preheat a 350°F/180°C/Gas 4 oven. Grease an 8 in (20 cm) baking dish.

2 ▲ In a frying pan, cook the bacon until browned and the fat is rendered. Drain the bacon on kitchen paper.

3 Add the onion to the bacon fat in the pan and cook until softened, about 5 minutes. Pour off excess fat.

4 ▲ Stir in the tomatoes and dried chilli peppers. Cook over high heat until thickened, about 10 minutes.

5 Meanwhile, cook the pasta in a large pan of boiling salted water until just tender (check packet instructions for timing). Drain well.

6 ▲ Put the pasta in a mixing bowl and add the bacon, tomato sauce, Mozzarella cheese and olives. Toss well to mix. Season to taste.

7 Cut the stem end off each pepper; reserve these 'lids'. Remove the seeds from inside the peppers and cut out the white ribs.

8 ▲ Divide the pasta mixture evenly among the peppers. Put on the "lids". Brush the peppers all over with the olive oil and set them in the prepared baking dish.

9 Cover the dish with foil and bake 30 minutes. Remove the foil and bake until the peppers are tender, 25–30 minutes longer.

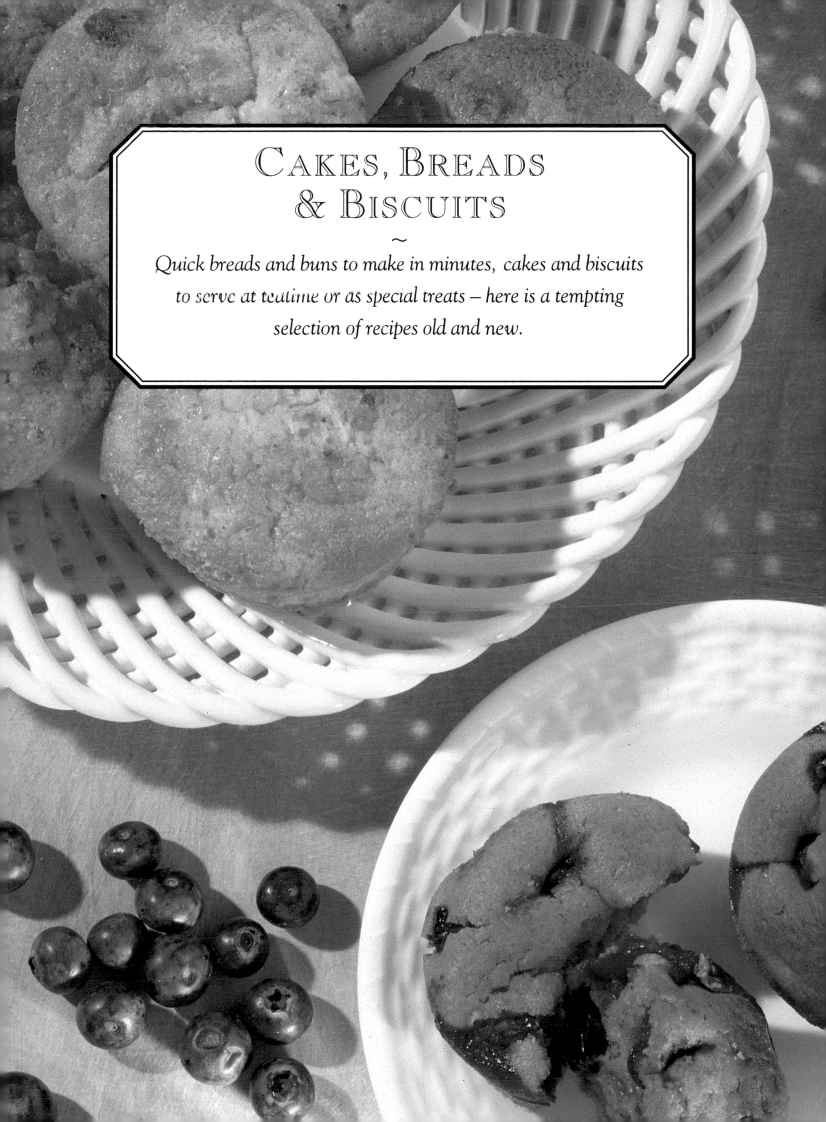

Cakes, Breads & Biscuits

~

Quick breads and buns to make in minutes, cakes and biscuits
to serve at teatime or as special treats – here is a tempting
selection of recipes old and new.

Ginger Cake with Spiced Whipped Cream

SERVES 9

6 oz (170 g) plain flour

2 tsp baking powder

½ tsp salt

2 tsp ground ginger

2 tsp ground cinnamon

1 tsp ground cloves

¼ tsp grated nutmeg

2 eggs

8 oz (225 g) caster sugar

8 fl oz (250 ml) whipping cream

1 tsp vanilla essence

icing sugar, for sprinkling

FOR THE SPICED WHIPPED CREAM

6 fl oz (175 ml) whipping cream

1 tsp icing sugar

¼ tsp ground cinnamon

¼ tsp ground ginger

⅛ tsp grated nutmeg

1 Preheat a 350°F/180°C/Gas 4 oven. Grease a 9 in (23 cm) square baking tin.

2 Sift the flour, baking powder, salt and spices into a bowl. Set aside.

3 ▲ With an electric mixer, beat the eggs on high speed until very thick, about 5 minutes. Gradually beat in the caster sugar.

4 ▲ With the mixer on low speed, beat in the flour mixture alternately with the cream, beginning and ending with the flour. Stir in the vanilla.

5 ▲ Pour the cake mixture into the tin and bake until the top springs back when touched lightly, 35–40 minutes. Let cool in the tin on a wire rack for 10 minutes.

6 ▲ Meanwhile, to make the spiced whipped cream, combine the ingredients in a bowl and whip until the cream will hold soft peaks.

7 Sprinkle icing sugar over the hot cake, cut in 9 squares, and serve with spiced whipped cream.

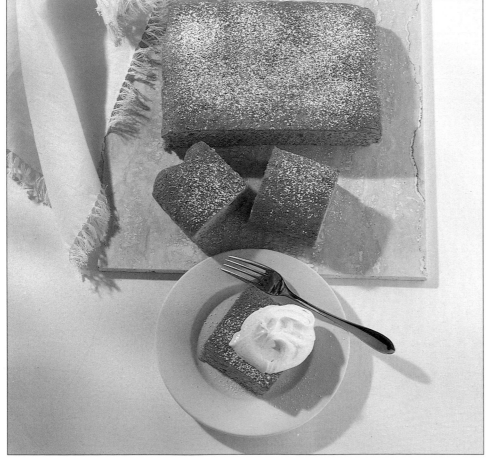

Madeira Cake

SERVES 12

8 oz (225 g) plain flour
1 tsp baking powder
8 oz (225 g) butter or margarine, at room temperature
8 oz (225 g) caster sugar
grated rind of 1 lemon
1 tsp vanilla essence
4 eggs

1 Preheat a 325°F/170°C/Gas 3 oven. Grease a 9 × 5 in (23 × 13 cm) loaf tin.

2 Sift the flour and baking powder into a small bowl. Set aside.

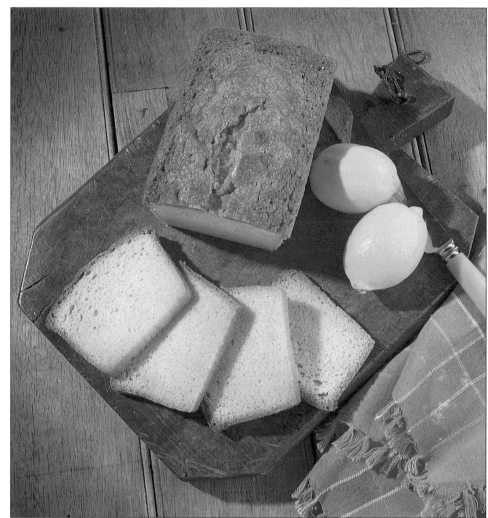

3 ▲ With an electric mixer, cream the butter or margarine, adding the sugar 2 tablespoons at a time, until light and fluffy. Stir in the lemon rind and vanilla.

5 ▼ Add the flour mixture and stir until just combined.

4 ▲ Add the eggs one at a time, beating for 1 minute after each addition.

6 ▲ Pour the cake mixture into the tin and tap lightly. Bake until a metal skewer inserted in the centre comes out clean, about 1¼ hours.

7 Let cool in the tin on a wire rack for 10 minutes, then unmould the cake from the tin onto the wire rack and let cool completely.

Strawberry Shortcake

SERVES 6

1 lb (450 g) strawberries, hulled and halved or quartered, depending on size
3 tbsp icing sugar
8 fl oz (250 ml) whipping cream
mint leaves, for garnishing
FOR THE SHORTCAKE
8 oz (225 g) plain flour
3 oz (85 g) caster sugar
1 tbsp baking powder
½ tsp salt
8 fl oz (250 ml) whipping cream

1 Preheat a 400°F/200°C/Gas 6 oven. Lightly grease a baking tray.

2 ▲ For the shortcake, sift the flour into a mixing bowl. Add 2 oz (55 g) of the caster sugar, the baking powder and salt. Stir well.

3 ▲ Gradually add the cream, tossing lightly with a fork until the mixture forms clumps.

4 ▲ Gather the clumps together, but do not knead the dough. Shape the dough into a 6 in (15 cm) log. Cut into 6 slices and place them on the prepared baking tray.

5 ▲ Sprinkle with the remaining 1 oz (30 g) caster sugar. Bake until light golden brown, about 15 minutes. Let cool on a wire rack.

6 ▲ Meanwhile, combine one-quarter of the strawberries with the icing sugar. Mash with a fork. Stir in the remaining strawberries. Let stand 1 hour at room temperature.

7 ▲ In a bowl, whip the cream until soft peaks form.

8 ▲ To serve, slice each shortcake in half horizontally using a serrated knife. Put the bottom halves on individual dessert plates. Top each half with some of the whipped cream. Divide the strawberries among the 6 shortcakes. Replace the tops and garnish with mint. Serve with the remaining whipped cream.

~ COOK'S TIP ~

For best results when whipping cream, refrigerate the bowl and beaters until thoroughly chilled. If using an electric mixer, increase speed gradually, and turn the bowl while beating to incorporate as much air as possible.

Apple Cake

SERVES 10

1½ lb (700 g) apples, peeled, cored and quartered

1 lb 2 oz (500 g) caster sugar

1 tbsp water

12 oz (350 g) plain flour

1¾ tsp bicarbonate of soda

1 tsp ground cinnamon

1 tsp ground cloves

6 oz (170 g) raisins

5 oz (140 g) chopped walnuts

8 oz (225 g) butter or margarine, at room temperature

1 tsp vanilla essence

FOR THE ICING

4 oz (115 g) icing sugar

¼ tsp vanilla essence

2–3 tbsp milk

1 ▲ Combine the apples, 2 oz (55 g) of the sugar and the water in a medium saucepan and bring to a boil. Simmer 25 minutes, stirring occasionally with a wooden spoon to break up any lumps. Let cool.

~ **COOK'S TIP** ~

Be sure to grease the cake tin generously and allow this cake to become completely cold before unmoulding it.

2 ▲ Preheat a 325°F/170°C/Gas 3 oven. Butter and flour a 3–3½ pt (1.75–2 litre) tube tin.

3 Sift the flour, bicarbonate of soda and spices into a mixing bowl. Remove 2 tablespoons of the mixture to a bowl and toss with the raisins and all but 1 oz (30 g) of the walnuts.

4 ▲ With an electric mixer, cream the butter or margarine and remaining sugar together until light and fluffy. Fold in the apple mixture gently with a wooden spoon.

5 ▲ Fold the flour mixture into the apple mixture. Stir in the vanilla and the raisin and walnut mixture.

6 Pour the cake mixture into the prepared tin. Bake until a skewer inserted in the centre comes out clean, about 1½ hours.

7 Let cool in the tin on a wire rack for 20 minutes, then unmould the cake from the tin onto the wire rack and let cool completely.

8 ▲ For the icing, put the sugar in a bowl and stir in the vanilla and 1 tablespoon of the milk. Add the remaining milk, teaspoon by teaspoon, until the icing is smooth and has a thick pouring consistency.

9 ▲ Transfer the cooled cake to a serving plate and drizzle the icing on top. Sprinkle with the remaining nuts. Let the cake stand for 2 hours before slicing, so the icing can set.

Banana and Nut Buns

MAKES 8

5 oz (140 g) plain flour

1½ tsp baking powder

2 oz (55 g) butter or margarine, at room
temperature

6 oz (170 g) caster sugar

1 egg

1 tsp vanilla essence

about 3 medium bananas, mashed

2 oz (55 g) chopped pecans

3 fl oz (85 ml) milk

~ VARIATION ~

Use an equal quantity of walnuts
instead of the pecans.

1 Preheat a 375°F/190°C/Gas 5 oven.
Grease a bun tray.

2 Sift the flour and baking powder
into a small bowl. Set aside.

3 ▲ With an electric mixer, cream
the butter or margarine and sugar
together. Add the egg and vanilla and
beat until fluffy. Mix in the banana.

4 ▼ Add the pecans. With the mixer
on low speed, beat in the flour
mixture alternately with the milk.

5 Spoon the mixture into the
prepared bun cups, filling them two-
thirds full. Bake until golden brown
and a skewer inserted into the centre
of a bun comes out clean, 20–25
minutes.

6 Let cool in the tray on a wire rack
for 10 minutes. To loosen, run a knife
gently around each bun and unmould
onto the wire rack. Let cool 10
minutes longer before serving.

Fruit and Cinnamon Buns

MAKES 8

4 oz (115 g) plain flour

1 tbsp baking powder

⅛ tsp salt

2½ oz (65 g) light brown sugar

1 egg

6 fl oz (175 ml) milk

3 tbsp vegetable oil

2 tsp ground cinnamon

5 oz (140 g) fresh or thawed frozen
blueberries, or blackcurrants

1 Preheat a 375°F/190°C/Gas 5 oven.
Grease a bun tray.

2 With an electric mixer, beat the
first 8 ingredients together until
smooth.

3 ▲ Fold in the blueberries or
blackcurrants.

4 ▲ Spoon the mixture into the bun
cups, filling them two-thirds full.
Bake until a skewer inserted in the
centre of a bun comes out clean, about
25 minutes.

5 Let cool in the bun tray on a wire
rack for 10 minutes, then unmould
the buns onto the wire rack and allow
to cool completely.

Banana and Nut Buns (top), Fruit and Cinnamon Buns

Lemon Squares

MAKES 12

8 oz (225 g) plain flour

2 oz (55 g) icing sugar

¼ tsp salt

6 oz (170 g) cold butter or margarine

1 tsp cold water

FOR THE LEMON LAYER

4 eggs

1 lb (450 g) caster sugar

1 oz (30 g) plain flour

½ tsp baking powder

1 tsp grated lemon rind

2 fl oz (65 ml) fresh lemon juice

icing sugar, for sprinkling

1 Preheat a 350°F/180°C/Gas 4 oven.

2 ▼ Sift the flour, icing sugar and salt into a mixing bowl. Using your fingertips or a pastry blender, rub or cut in the butter or margarine until the mixture resembles coarse breadcrumbs. Add the water and toss lightly with a fork until the mixture forms a ball.

3 ▲ Press the mixture evenly into an ungreased 13 × 9 in (33 × 23 cm) baking dish. Bake until light golden brown, 15–20 minutes. Remove from oven and let cool slightly.

4 Meanwhile, with an electric mixer, beat together the eggs, caster sugar, flour, baking powder and lemon rind and juice.

5 ▲ Pour the lemon mixture over the baked base. Return to the oven and bake 25 minutes. Let cool, in the baking dish, on a wire rack.

6 ▲ Before serving, sprinkle the top with icing sugar. Cut into squares with a sharp knife.

Chocolate Chip Nut Biscuits

MAKES 36

4 oz (115 g) plain flour

1 tsp baking powder

¼ tsp salt

3 oz (85 g) butter or margarine, at room temperature

4 oz (115 g) caster sugar

1¾ oz (50 g) light brown sugar

1 egg

1 tsp vanilla essence

4½ oz (130 g) chocolate chips

2 oz (55 g) hazelnuts, chopped

1 ▲ Preheat a 350°F/180°C/Gas 4 oven. Grease 2–3 baking trays.

2 Sift the flour, baking powder and salt into a small bowl. Set aside.

3 ▲ With an electric mixer, cream the butter or margarine and sugars together. Beat in the egg and vanilla.

4 Add the flour mixture and beat well with the mixer on low speed.

5 ▼ Stir in the chocolate chips and half of the hazelnuts using a wooden spoon.

6 Drop teaspoonfuls of the mixture onto the prepared baking trays, to form ¾ in (2 cm) mounds. Space the biscuits 1–2 in (2–5 cm) apart.

7 ▲ Flatten each biscuit lightly with a wet fork. Sprinkle the remaining hazelnuts on top of the biscuits and press lightly into the surface.

8 Bake until golden brown, about 10–12 minutes. With a slotted spatula, transfer the biscuits to a wire rack and let cool.

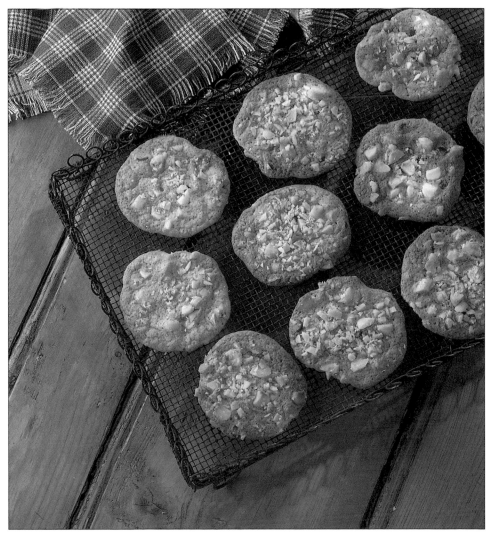

Buttermilk Scones

MAKES 10

8 oz (225 g) plain flour

1 tsp baking powder

½ tsp bicarbonate of soda

1 tsp salt

2 oz (55 g) butter or margarine, chilled

6 fl oz (175 ml) buttermilk

~ COOK'S TIP ~

If time is short, drop heaped tablespoonfuls of the biscuit mixture onto the baking tray without kneading or cutting it out.

---

1 Preheat a 425°F/220°C/Gas 7 oven.

2 ▼ Sift the flour, baking powder, bicarbonate of soda and salt into a mixing bowl. Cut in the butter or margarine with a fork until the mixture resembles coarse breadcrumbs.

3 ▲ Add the buttermilk and mix until well combined to a soft dough.

4 ▲ Turn the dough onto a lightly floured board and knead 30 seconds.

5 ▲ Roll out the dough to ½ in (1 cm) thickness. Use a floured 2½ in (6 cm) pastry cutter to cut out rounds.

6 Transfer the rounds to a baking tray and bake until golden brown, 10–12 minutes. Serve hot.

Savoury Parmesan Puddings

MAKES 6

8 tbsp freshly grated Parmesan cheese
4 oz (115 g) plain flour
¼ tsp salt
2 eggs
8 fl oz (250 ml) milk
1 tbsp butter or margarine, melted

1 ▼ Preheat a 450°F/230°C/Gas 8 oven. Grease 6 individual baking tins. Sprinkle each pan with 1 tablespoon of the grated Parmesan. Alternatively, you can use ramekins, in which case, heat them on a baking tray in the oven, then grease and sprinkle with Parmesan just before filling.

2 Sift the flour and salt into a small bowl. Set aside.

3 ▲ In a mixing bowl, beat together the eggs, milk and butter or margarine. Add the flour mixture and stir until smoothly blended.

4 ▼ Divide the batter evenly among the containers, filling each one about half full. Bake for 15 minutes, then sprinkle the tops of the puddings with the remaining grated Parmesan cheese. Reduce the heat to 350°F/180°C/Gas 4 and continue baking until the puddings are firm and golden brown, 20–25 minutes.

5 ▲ Remove the puddings from the oven. To unmould, run a thin knife around the inside of each tin to loosen them. Gently ease out, then transfer to a wire rack to cool.

Sweet Potato and Raisin Bread

MAKES 1

10 oz (300 g) plain flour
2 tsp baking powder
½ tsp salt
1 tsp ground cinnamon
½ tsp grated nutmeg
1 lb (450 g) mashed cooked sweet potatoes
3½ oz (100 g) light brown sugar
4 oz (115 g) butter or margarine, melted and cooled
3 eggs, beaten
3 oz (85 g) raisins

1 ▼ Preheat a 350°F/180°C/Gas 4 oven. Grease a 9 × 5 in (23 × 13 cm) loaf tin.

2 Sift the flour, baking powder, salt, cinnamon and nutmeg into a small bowl. Set aside.

3 ▼ With an electric mixer, beat the mashed sweet potatoes with the brown sugar, butter or margarine and eggs until well mixed.

4 ▼ Add the flour mixture and the raisins. Stir with a wooden spoon until the flour is just mixed in.

5 ▲ Transfer the batter to the prepared tin. Bake until a skewer inserted in the centre comes out clean, 1–1¼ hours.

6 Let cool in the tin on a wire rack for 15 minutes, then unmould the bread from the tin onto the wire rack and let cool completely.

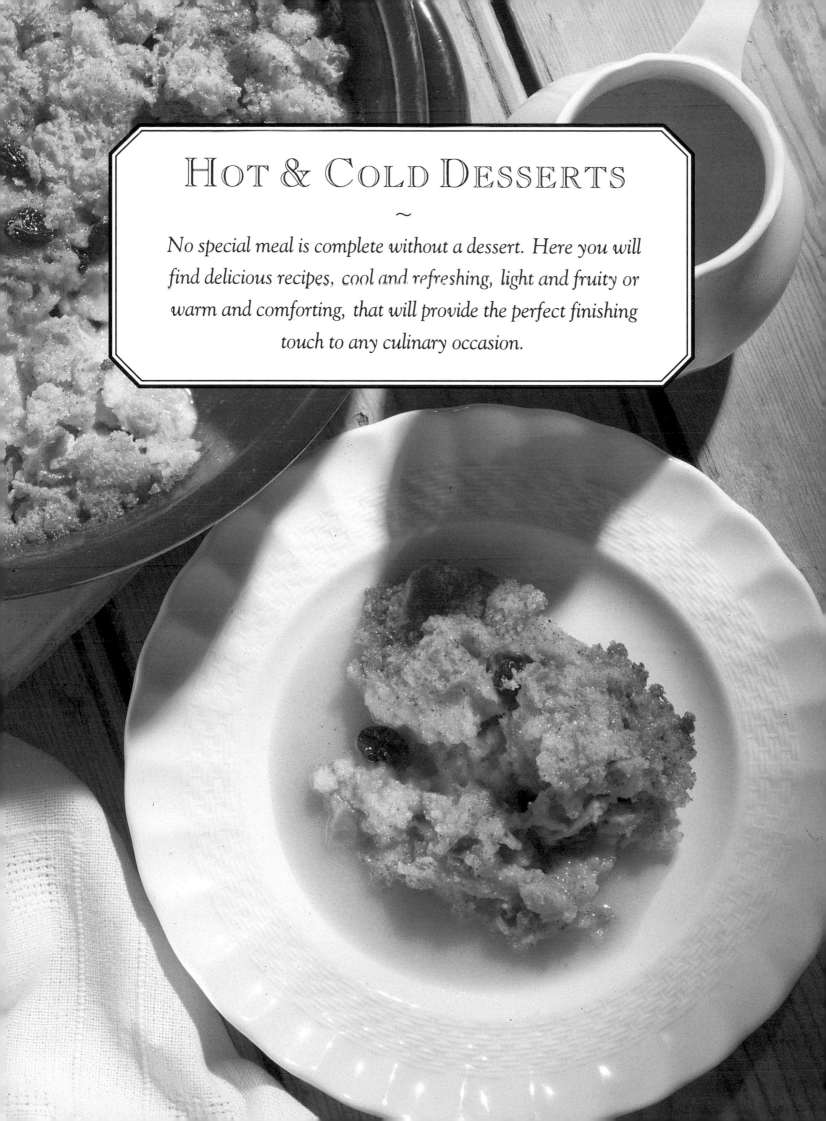

Hot & Cold Desserts

~

No special meal is complete without a dessert. Here you will find delicious recipes, cool and refreshing, light and fruity or warm and comforting, that will provide the perfect finishing touch to any culinary occasion.

Hot Spiced Bananas

SERVES 6

6 ripe bananas

7 oz (200 g) light brown sugar

8 fl oz (250 ml) unsweetened pineapple juice

4 fl oz (125 ml) dark rum

2 cinnamon sticks

12 whole cloves

1 ▼ Preheat a 350°F/180°C/Gas 4 oven. Grease a 9 in (23 cm) baking dish.

2 ▲ Peel the bananas and cut them into 1 in (2.5 cm) pieces on the diagonal. Arrange the banana pieces evenly over the bottom of the prepared baking dish.

3 ▲ In a saucepan, combine the sugar and pineapple juice. Cook over a medium heat until the sugar has dissolved, stirring occasionally.

4 Add the rum, cinnamon sticks and cloves. Bring to the boil, then remove the pan from the heat.

5 ▲ Pour the pineapple and spice mixture over the bananas. Bake until the bananas are very tender and hot, 25–30 minutes. Serve hot.

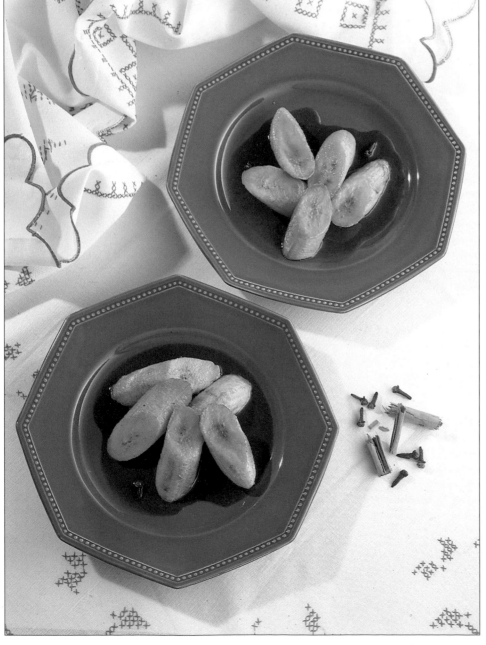

Apple and Walnut Crisp

SERVES 6

about 2 lb (900 g) tart eating apples, such as Granny Smith, peeled, cored and sliced
grated rind of ½ lemon
1 tbsp fresh lemon juice
3½ oz (100 g) light brown sugar
3 oz (85 g) plain flour
¼ tsp salt
¼ tsp grated nutmeg
½ tsp ground cardamom
½ tsp ground cinnamon
4 oz (115 g) butter or margarine, diced
2 oz (55 g) chopped walnuts

1 Preheat a 350°F/180°C/Gas 4 oven. Grease a 9–10 in (23–25 cm) oval gratin dish or shallow baking dish.

2 ▲ Toss the apples with the lemon rind and juice. Arrange them evenly in the bottom of the prepared dish.

3 In a mixing bowl, combine the brown sugar, flour, salt, nutmeg, cardamom and cinnamon. With 2 knives, or a pastry blender, cut in the butter or margarine until the mixture resembles coarse breadcrumbs. Mix in the walnuts.

4 ▼ With a spoon, sprinkle the walnut and spice mixture evenly over the apples. Cover with foil and bake for 30 minutes.

5 ▲ Remove the foil and continue baking until the apples are tender and the topping is crisp, about 30 minutes longer. Serve warm.

Bread Pudding with Whiskey Sauce

SERVES 8

about 6 oz (170 g) stale French bread, in ¾ in (2 cm) cubes
16 fl oz (450 ml) milk
2 eggs
8 oz (225 g) caster sugar
1 tbsp vanilla essence
½ tsp ground cinnamon
¼ tsp grated nutmeg
2 oz (55 g) butter or margarine, melted and cooled slightly
3 oz (85 g) raisins
FOR THE SAUCE
2 egg yolks
4 oz (115 g) butter or margarine
8 oz (225 g) sugar
3 fl oz (85 ml) bourbon or Irish whiskey

1 ▲ Preheat a 350°F/180°C/Gas 4 oven. Grease an 8 in (20 cm) baking dish.

2 ▲ Put the bread cubes in a bowl with the milk and squeeze the bread with your hands until well saturated.

3 ▲ With an electric mixer on high speed, beat the eggs with the sugar until pale and thick. Stir in the vanilla, cinnamon, nutmeg, butter or margarine and raisins.

4 ▲ Add the soaked bread cube mixture and stir well to mix. Let stand 10 minutes.

5 ▲ Transfer the mixture to the prepared baking dish. Bake until firm and a knife inserted in the middle comes out clean, 45–50 minutes. Let it cool slightly in the dish, set on a wire rack.

6 ▲ Meanwhile, make the sauce. With an electric mixer, beat the egg yolks until thick and pale.

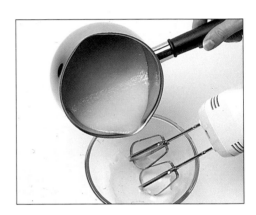

7 ▲ Melt the butter or margarine and sugar in a saucepan. Pour the butter and sugar mixture over the egg yolks, beating constantly, until well thickened. Stir in the whiskey.

8 Serve the warm pudding from its baking dish. Pass the hot whiskey sauce separately.

~ COOK'S TIP ~

It is important to allow enough time for the egg mixture to soak the bread thoroughly; otherwise the bread cubes will float on top, leaving a layer of custard on the bottom when the dish is cooked.

Spiced Milk Pudding

Serves 6

1¾ pt (1 litre) milk
1½ oz (45 g) semolina
½ tsp salt
¼ tsp ground ginger
¾ tsp ground cinnamon
2 oz (55 g) butter or margarine
8 fl oz (250 ml) treacle
2 eggs, beaten

1 Heat three-quarters of the milk in a saucepan.

2 In a heatproof bowl set over a pan of boiling water, or in a double boiler, combine the semolina, salt, ginger, cinnamon and remaining milk.

3 ▼ Pour in the heated milk, stirring to combine. Cook, stirring constantly, until smooth.

4 Reduce the heat so the water is just simmering, and cook 25 minutes, stirring frequently.

5 Preheat a 350°F/180°C/Gas 4 oven. Grease a deep 1¾ pt (1 litre) earthenware baking dish.

6 ▲ Remove the bowl from the heat. Stir in the butter or margarine and treacle until the mixture is smooth. Stir in the eggs.

7 Pour the mixture into the prepared baking dish. Bake 1 hour. Serve warm.

Lemon Sponge Pudding

Serves 6

4 oz (115 g) plain flour
1 tsp baking powder
¼ + ⅛ tsp salt
4 oz (115 g) butter or margarine, at room temperature
10 oz (300 g) caster sugar
finely grated rind and juice of 4 large lemons
4 eggs, separated
10 fl oz (300 ml) milk

1 Preheat a 350°F/180°C/Gas 4 oven. Butter a 10 in (25 cm) baking dish.

2 Sift the flour, baking powder and ¼ teaspoon salt into a small bowl. Set aside.

3 ▼ With an electric mixer, beat together the butter or margarine, sugar and lemon rind. Beat in the egg yolks, one at a time. Mix in the flour mixture alternately with the milk and lemon juice (reserving a squeeze of juice), beginning and ending with the flour.

4 ▲ In a clean bowl, beat the egg whites with the ⅛ teaspoon salt and squeeze of lemon juice until stiff peaks form. Fold into the lemon mixture.

5 Pour into the prepared baking dish. Bake until golden brown, 40–45 minutes. Serve hot.

Spiced Milk Pudding (top), Lemon Sponge Pudding

Traditional Apple Pie

SERVES 8

about 2 lb (900 g) tart eating apples, such as Granny Smith, peeled, cored and sliced

1 tbsp fresh lemon juice

1 tsp vanilla essence

4 oz (115 g) caster sugar

½ tsp ground cinnamon

1½ oz (45 g) butter or margarine

1 egg yolk

2 tsp whipping cream

FOR THE PASTRY

8 oz (225 g) plain flour

1 tsp salt

6 oz (170 g) lard or vegetable fat

4–5 tbsp iced water

1 tbsp quick-cooking tapioca

1 Preheat a 450°F/230°C/Gas 8 oven.

2 For the pastry, sift the flour and salt into a bowl. Using a pastry blender, cut in the fat until the mixture resembles coarse breadcrumbs.

3 ▲ Sprinkle in the water, 1 tablespoon at a time, tossing lightly with your fingertips or with a fork until the pastry forms a ball.

4 ▲ Divide the pastry in half and shape each half into a ball. On a lightly floured surface, roll out one of the balls to a circle about 12 in (30 cm) in diameter.

5 ▲ Use it to line a 9 in (23 cm) pie tin, easing the dough in and being careful not to stretch it. Trim off the excess pastry and use the trimmings for decorating. Sprinkle the tapioca over the bottom of the pie shell.

6 ▲ Roll out the remaining pastry to ⅛ in (3 mm) thickness. With a sharp knife, cut out 8 large leaf-shapes. Cut the trimmings into small leaf shapes. Score the leaves with the back of the knife to mark veins.

7 ▲ In a bowl, toss the apples with the lemon juice, vanilla, sugar and cinnamon. Fill the pastry case with the apple mixture and dot with the butter or margarine.

8 ▲ Arrange the large pastry leaves in a decorative pattern on top. Decorate the edge with small leaves.

9 ▲ Mix together the egg yolk and cream and brush over the leaves to glaze them.

10 Bake 10 minutes, then reduce the heat to 350°F/180°C/Gas 4 and continue baking until the pastry is golden brown, 35–45 minutes. Let the pie cool in the tin, set on a wire rack.

Pumpkin Pie

Serves 8

about 9 oz (250 g) puréed pumpkin

16 fl oz (450 ml) single cream

4½ oz (135 g) light brown sugar

¼ tsp salt

1 tsp ground cinnamon

½ tsp ground ginger

¼ tsp ground cloves

⅛ tsp grated nutmeg

2 eggs

FOR THE PASTRY

5½ oz (165 g) plain flour

½ tsp salt

4 oz (115 g) lard or vegetable fat

2–3 tbsp iced water

1½ oz (45 g) pecans, chopped

1 Preheat a 425°F/220°C/Gas 7 oven.

2 ▲ For the pastry, sift the flour and salt into a mixing bowl. Using a pastry blender, cut in the fat until the mixture resembles coarse breadcrumbs. Sprinkle in the water, 1 tablespoon at a time, tossing lightly with a fork until the mixture forms a ball.

3 ▲ On a lightly floured surface, roll out the pastry to ¼ in (5 mm) thickness. Use it to line a 9 in (23 cm) pie tin. Ease the pastry in without stretching it. Trim off the excess.

4 ▲ If you like, use the pastry trimmings to make a decorative rope edge. Cut in strips and twist together in pairs. Dampen the rim of the pastry case and press on the rope edge. Or, with your thumbs, make a fluted edge. Sprinkle the chopped pecans over the bottom of the case.

5 With a whisk or an electric mixer on medium speed, beat together the puréed pumpkin, cream, brown sugar, salt, spices and eggs.

6 Pour the pumpkin mixture into the pastry case. Bake 10 minutes, then reduce the heat to 350°F/180°C/Gas 4 and continue baking until the filling is set, about 45 minutes. Let the pie cool in the tin, set on a wire rack.

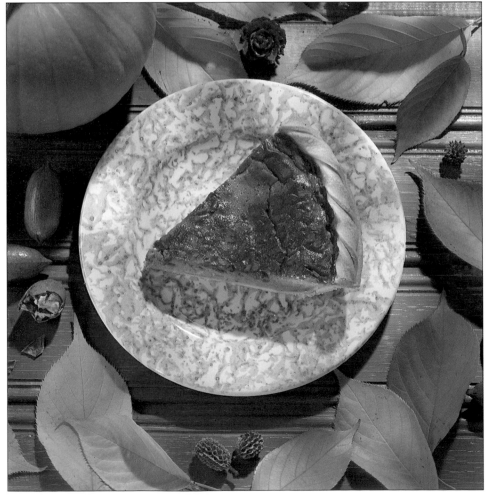

Maple Syrup and Pecan Pie

SERVES 8

3 eggs, beaten
3½ oz (100 g) dark brown sugar
5 fl oz (150 ml) golden syrup
3 fl oz (85 ml) maple syrup
½ tsp vanilla essence
⅛ tsp salt
4 oz (115 g) pecan halves
FOR THE PASTRY
5½ oz (165 g) plain flour
½ tsp salt
1 tsp ground cinnamon
4 oz (115 g) lard or vegetable fat
2–3 tbsp iced water

1 Preheat a 425°F/220°C/Gas 7 oven.

2 For the pastry, sift the flour, salt and cinnamon into a mixing bowl. Using a pastry blender, cut in the fat until the mixture resembles coarse breadcrumbs. Sprinkle in the water, 1 tablespoon at a time, tossing lightly with your fingertips or a fork until the mixture forms a ball.

3 On a lightly floured surface, roll out the pastry to a circle 15 in (38 cm) in diameter. Use it to line a 9 in (23 cm) pie tin, easing in the pastry and being careful not to stretch it.

4 ▲ With your thumbs, make a fluted edge. Using a fork, prick the bottom and sides of the pastry case all over. Bake until lightly browned, 10–15 minutes. Let cool in the tin.

5 ▼ Reduce the oven temperature to 350°F/180°C/Gas 4. In a bowl, stir together the eggs, sugar, syrups, vanilla and salt until well mixed.

6 ▲ Sprinkle the pecans evenly over the bottom of the baked pastry case. Pour in the egg mixture. Bake until the filling is set and the pastry is golden brown, about 40 minutes. Let cool in the tin, set on a wire rack.

Lime Meringue Pie

SERVES 8

3 egg yolks

12 fl oz (350 ml) sweetened condensed milk

finely grated rind and juice of 4 limes

7 egg whites

⅛ tsp salt

squeeze of fresh lemon juice

4 oz (115 g) sugar

½ tsp vanilla essence

FOR THE PASTRY

5½ oz (165 g) plain flour

½ tsp salt

4 oz (115 g) lard or vegetable fat

2–3 tbsp iced water

1 Preheat a 425°F/220°C/Gas 7 oven.

2 ▲ For the pastry, sift the flour and salt into a mixing bowl. Using a pastry blender or 2 knives, cut in the fat until the mixture resembles coarse breadcrumbs. Sprinkle in the water, 1 tablespoon at a time, tossing lightly with a fork until the mixture forms a ball.

~ **COOK'S TIP** ~

When beating egg whites with an electric mixer, start slowly, and increase speed after they become frothy. Turn the bowl constantly.

3 ▲ On a lightly floured surface, roll out the pastry. Use it to line a 9 in (23 cm) pie tin, easing in the pastry. Make a fluted edge.

4 Using a fork, prick the bottom and sides of the pastry case all over. Bake until lightly browned, 10–15 minutes. Let cool, in the tin, on a wire rack. Reduce oven temperature to 350°F/180°C/Gas 4.

5 ▲ With an electric mixer on high speed, beat the yolks and condensed milk. Stir in the lime rind and juice.

6 ▲ In another clean bowl, beat 3 of the egg whites until stiff. Fold into the lime mixture.

7 ▲ Spread the lime filling in the pastry case. Bake 10 minutes.

8 ▲ Meanwhile, beat the remaining egg whites with the salt and lemon juice until soft peaks form. Beat in the sugar, 1 tablespoon at a time, until stiff peaks form. Add the vanilla.

9 ▲ Remove the pie from the oven. Using a metal spatula, spread the meringue over the lime filling, making a swirled design and covering the surface completely.

10 Bake until the meringue is lightly browned and the pastry is golden brown, about 12 minutes longer. Let cool, in the tin, on a wire rack.

Fruit Kebabs with Mango and Yoghurt Sauce

Serves 4

½ pineapple, peeled, cored and cubed

2 kiwi fruit, peeled and cubed

5 oz (140 g) strawberries, hulled and cut in half lengthwise, if large

½ mango, peeled, stoned and cubed

For the sauce

4 fl oz (125 ml) fresh mango purée, from 1–1½ peeled and stoned mangoes

4 fl oz (125 ml) thick plain yoghurt

1 tsp sugar

⅛ tsp vanilla essence

1 tbsp finely shredded fresh mint leaves

1 To make the sauce, beat together the mango purée, yoghurt, sugar and vanilla with an electric mixer.

2 ▼ Stir in the mint. Cover the sauce and refrigerate until required.

3 ▲ Thread the fruit onto 12 × 6 in (15 cm) wooden skewers, alternating the pineapple, kiwi fruit, strawberries and mango cubes.

4 Arrange the kebabs on a large serving platter with the mango and yoghurt sauce in the centre.

Tropical Fruits in Cinnamon Syrup

Serves 6

1 lb (450 g) caster sugar

1 cinnamon stick

1 large or 2 medium papayas (about 1½ lb/700 g), peeled, seeded and cut lengthwise into thin pieces

1 large or 2 medium mangoes (about 1½ lb/700 g), peeled, stoned and cut lengthwise into thin pieces

1 large or 2 small starfruit (about 8 oz/ 225 g), thinly sliced

1 Sprinkle one-third of the sugar over the bottom of a large saucepan. Add the cinnamon stick and half the papaya, mango and starfruit pieces.

> ~ **COOK'S TIP** ~
>
> Starfruit is sometimes called carambola.

2 ▼ Sprinkle half of the remaining sugar over the fruit pieces in the pan. Add the remaining fruit and sprinkle with the remaining sugar.

3 Cover the pan and cook the fruit over medium-low heat until the sugar dissolves completely, 35–45 minutes. Shake the pan occasionally, but do not stir or the fruit will collapse.

4 ▲ Uncover the pan and simmer until the fruit begins to appear translucent, about 10 minutes. Remove the pan from the heat and let stand to cool. Remove the cinnamon stick.

5 Transfer the fruit and syrup to a bowl, cover and refrigerate overnight.

Fruit Kebabs with Mango and Yoghurt Sauce (top), Tropical Fruits in Cinnamon Syrup

Italian Trifles

SERVES 4

8 oz (225 g) mascarpone cheese

1½ tbsp caster sugar

2 eggs, at room temperature, separated

⅛ tsp salt

squeeze of fresh lemon juice

4 fl oz (125 ml) very strong cold black coffee

2 tbsp coffee liqueur

4 oz (115 g) biscuits, macaroons or Madeira cake, coarsely crumbled

2 tbsp cocoa powder, sifted

~ **COOK'S TIP** ~

Buying very fresh eggs from a reputable producer is especially important when using them raw.

---

1 With an electric mixer, beat the cheese, sugar and egg yolks together until blended and creamy.

2 ▲ In a clean mixing bowl, beat the egg whites with the salt and lemon juice until stiff peaks form. Fold into the cheese mixture.

3 In a small bowl, combine the coffee and liqueur.

4 ▲ Divide half the crushed biscuits among 4 stemmed glasses. Drizzle over 1–1½ tablespoons of the liqueur mixture. Top the moistened biscuits with half the mascarpone mixture. Layer the remaining biscuits, coffee mixture and mascarpone mixture in the same way.

5 Cover and refrigerate the desserts for 1–2 hours. Sprinkle with the sifted cocoa powder before serving.

White Chocolate Mousse

SERVES 8

9 oz (250 g) white chocolate

3 fl oz (85 ml) milk

12 fl oz (350 ml) whipping cream

1 tsp vanilla essence

3 egg whites, at room temperature

⅛ tsp salt

squeeze of fresh lemon juice

chocolate covered coffee beans, for decoration (optional)

1 In a heatproof bowl set over a pan of barely simmering water, or in a double boiler, melt the chocolate.

2 Scald the milk in a small saucepan. Remove the bowl of chocolate from the heat and whisk in the warm milk until smooth. Let cool.

3 In a mixing bowl, whip the cream with the vanilla until soft peaks form. Refrigerate until needed.

4 ▲ Using an electric mixer and a clean bowl, beat the egg whites with the salt and lemon juice until stiff peaks form (do not overbeat or the mousse will be grainy). Fold into the chocolate mixture.

5 ▲ Gently fold the chocolate and egg white mixture into the vanilla flavoured whipped cream.

6 Transfer to a pretty serving bowl or individual stemmed glasses. Cover and refrigerate at least 1 hour. Sprinkle with chocolate covered coffee beans before serving, if wished.

Italian Trifles (top), White Chocolate Mousse

Coffee Ice Cream Sandwiches

MAKES 8

4 oz (115 g) butter or margarine, at room temperature

2 oz (55 g) caster sugar

4 oz (115 g) plain flour

2 tbsp instant coffee

icing sugar, for sprinkling

16 fl oz (450 ml) coffee ice cream

2 tbsp cocoa powder, for sprinkling

1 Lightly grease 2–3 baking trays.

2 With an electric mixer or wooden spoon, beat the butter or margarine until soft. Beat in the caster sugar.

3 ▲ Add the flour and coffee and mix by hand to form an evenly blended dough. Wrap in a plastic bag and refrigerate at least 1 hour.

4 Lightly sprinkle the work surface with icing sugar. Knead the dough on the sugared surface for a few minutes to soften it slightly.

5 ▼ Using a rolling pin dusted with icing sugar, roll out the dough to ⅛ in (3 mm) thickness. With a 2½ in (6 cm) fluted pastry cutter, cut out 16 rounds. Transfer the rounds to the prepared baking trays. Refrigerate for at least 30 minutes.

6 Preheat a 300°F/150°C/Gas 2 oven. Bake the biscuits until they are lightly golden, about 30 minutes. Let them cool and firm up before removing them from the trays to a wire rack to cool completely.

7 Remove the ice cream from the freezer and let soften 10 minutes at room temperature.

8 ▲ With a metal spatula, spread the ice cream evenly on the flat side of eight of the biscuits, leaving the edges clear. Top with the remaining biscuits, flat-side down.

9 Arrange the ice cream sandwiches on a baking tray. Cover and freeze at least 1 hour, longer if a firmer sandwich is desired. Sift the cocoa powder over the tops before serving.

INDEX

~